Esther Rantzen

Older &
Bolder

My A-Z of surviving almost everything

Illustrated by Joel Stewart

EBURY
SPOTLIGHT

To my children Miriam, Rebecca and Joshua,
thanking them for their love, support and
incredible tolerance.

Contents

Introduction

A is for Advice, and this book is crammed with advice, gleaned from my own experience – what I've learned as a journalist, author and broadcaster – and from what I've been told on the rare occasions when I've actually listened to somebody else who turned out to be worth hearing.

As you will discover, I never hold back on handing out advice. Except with my family. After all, at my age I have so much life experience the world needs to learn from. If I see someone in the wrong clothes, wearing the wrong make-up or spouting woke rubbish, I tell them so. They'll ignore you anyway if you are not an 'influencer' or reality star.

But forget the family – they've been hearing this stuff all their lives and you'll repeat yourself so often they may decide you've lost it and do something draconian like power of attorney.

Ageing

As Bette Davis said, old age ain't no place for sissies. As you grow older you need to be bolder to cope with the many changes that arrive unexpectedly in your life and around your body – your earlobes put on weight so the favourite earrings don't fit any more, your feet shrink, insomnia strikes so you have to find some way of passing the hours between 3 and 4am since you have run out of the energy, and the company, to do anything more strenuous in bed than Wordle.

But there are also unexpected advantages. For instance, you no longer have to impress anyone else by pretending to enjoy something that bores you. In my case, that is bad productions of grand opera. Obviously, I love Mozart at Glyndebourne, who wouldn't? But fat people shouting that they are dying, still dying, haven't died yet, to an audience of people who are only there to impress other people: enough already.

I used to go to Covent Garden to hear singers who had just flown into Heathrow from some opera house abroad: they had no idea what was happening onstage, could barely recognise the conductor, sang the part they had just sung in New York or Milan, and then left on the next plane for the next opera house. I went to a production of *Otello* in Venice where Desdemona was so huge and Otello was so tiny that seeing him trying to strangle her was like watching someone climbing Everest: she could have flicked him off with one finger. Either go to the opera house to listen with your eyes shut or stay home and buy a record.

Allergies

Nobody ever warns you that as time goes by for some reason you develop brand new allergies – in my case I am suddenly allergic to champagne. How cruel is that? And to people, too. Because when you know you have limited time left, why spend it with people who annoy you? But I was advised by an expert that in old age you do need to burnish the links you made when young, with friends and family, because you will need them if you lose mobility or the lawn needs mowing.

Anger

Give it up, if you can: anger takes too much energy and can lead to bad decision-making. In 2010 I was so furious about the scandal of MPs' expenses I decided to stand for Parliament myself, as an independent candidate in Luton South. That just led to my being derided by the *Daily Mail*, beaten up on *Moral Maze* and by Paxman on *Newsnight*, and losing my deposit. So I ended up bruised psychologi-cally and financially.

But at least it taught me two valuable lessons: firstly, as my coffee mug advises, keep calm and carry on. Secondly, when I walked around knocking on people's doors: how many people spend the day at home stark naked. At least in Luton.

Antihistamines

Take them to combat allergies. They work well against hay fever but not against people.

April Fools

I've always loved what we used to call practical jokes, and what are now called pranks, so April the first is one of my favourite days of the year. Especially when we were making *That's Life!* and we broadcast on that mischievous date, which happened three times in our 21-year run. There is some stupid made-up rule that claims you can only prank people before noon. Rubbish. *Panorama* famously showed their film of spaghetti being harvested from Italian trees at eight in the evening; we broadcast ours at nine on Sunday nights, and revelled in tricking our viewers.

Our first and most famous April Fool film was a driving dog; it was directed by the brilliant Nick Handel. Because we had already filmed series of extraordinarily talented dogs that could talk, read, play the piano, sing and play football, Nick was heartily sick of them. So I promised him revenge with this April Fool and he threw himself into it.

My A–Z of surviving almost everything

Nick cleverly combined close-ups of a real Old English sheepdog with wide shots of a lady inside a shaggy dog costume. Reporter Chris Serle recruited a friend of his with an enviable deadpan face to play the dog owner, and off they went in a car on a low loader, fascinating dogs they drove past and alarming cyclists. It was sheer joy. The film ended with them being flagged down by an actor playing a policeman who demanded they accompany him back to the police station, at which point the owner encouraged the dog to accelerate away, leaving him gesticulating at the roadside, with the owner explaining, 'What can he possibly say when he gets back to the station?' The BBC's switchboard was swamped with complaints from viewers at the appalling way the officer was treated, and the danger the driving dog posed to other traffic. We were delighted.

Our second April Fool film was an exposé of a face cream that removed wrinkles from your face but transferred them to your backside. The magic ingredient that achieved this effect (which sadly put some marriages at risk) was rhinoceros spit. To the best of my knowledge rhinos don't spit, or at any rate don't spit enough to fill the tanker we showed pulling up outside the gates of London Zoo to collect hundreds of gallons of it. When we illustrated our film with library footage of rhinos grazing on the savannah, our film director Tom dubbed his own revolting throat-clearing and spitting onto the soundtrack as evidence. So please, please do not believe everything you see and hear on television.

My cousin, a doctor, told me that the day after it broadcast, his fellow consultants met over coffee in the hospital and discussed possible explanations as to why the wrinkles migrated from face to bum, and they suggested there must be special rhino hormones. My cousin, who had met me before, mentioned the date, but they ignored him.

Our third prank film came from an idea suggested by one of the curators at London Zoo, who suggested we could invent an animal called the Lirpa Loof. So we did, a little hairy beast with purple droppings (made by the BBC's special effects department) and which imitated visitors: when they pointed at him, he pointed back. Charabancs of children arrived at the zoo the next day asking where the Lirpa was, but he had disappeared.

I wonder if April Fools belong to a past golden age, when respect held sway, and irreverence was limited to one day a year. Maybe you have to be serious to make jokes. Nowadays, when TV series proliferate with celebrities and

My A–Z of surviving almost everything

ordinary people being deceived and tricked, and their humiliation recorded on hidden cameras, pranks like ours would not be events any more. I recently assisted a BBC programme to create an April Fool film claiming that Prince Albert, Queen Victoria's husband, was a secret nudist. I collected all kinds of evidence, including a revealing statue of him which Victoria loved but which was considered so shocking it was relegated to their holiday home, Osborne House on the Isle of Wight. There was no comment from the royal family when it broadcast, or from anyone else. If anyone did realise it was an April Fool, nobody accused me.

For me, the funniest moment was when we were making the film and asked permission to interview one of our experts, Professor Dame Mary Beard, in Apsley House, where there is a gigantic statue of Napoleon in the nude, so I could claim that was Prince Albert's inspiration. The current Duke of Wellington (or to be properly respectful, His Grace and Serene Highness Charles Duke of Wellington), GE, OBE, DL, who owns the house, refused. The very idea is still too shocking, though whether the Duke was objecting to nudity, or to making a joke about royalty, I don't know. Nice to shock somebody at my great age.

Architects and Surveyors

Whatever kind of property you buy, or build, or extend, use a properly qualified architect. A mortgage survey is not enough. I decided to buy a bigger flat in my block, and as my current flat was structurally fine, it didn't occur to me that I needed a proper survey. Until a friend noticed there was blistering on the laminated floor, I got a surveyor in, and he told me his damp meter was off the chart. Turns out there was a leak which had created a huge lake under the floorboards so they had to demolish all the internal walls to find the source and dam it. Which was embarrassing, as I was in the middle of buying the flat from another friend. Don't do that either.

Arithmetic

Leave it to accountants. Nobody is great at everything, except Leonardo da Vinci and even he may not have been terrific at knitting or peeling potatoes. He was left-handed like me, and I've never been able to do either. So the trick is, as doubtless Leonardo discovered, to find someone who can. I've always done the same with numbers. As I have never been numerate, I find filling out tax forms totally impossible, so I have an accountant who does it.

The other useful trick is to advise your daughter to marry an accountant, as one of my daughters did. Not that she asked me for guidance, but had she done so, that would have been my advice. Odd the way mothers are not consulted in romantic matters, although my husband did propose to my mother before he proposed to me. She accepted. On my behalf.

Arrest

One day, when I was handing out bat stew in the streets of London for a consumer test for *That's Life!* (wouldn't be allowed today, either for conservation or for Covid-19 reasons), a policeman appeared, accused me of obstruction, and arrested me. This is all available on film and causes some hilarity, because I was so unfamiliar with being arrested that I climbed into the front seat of the Black

Maria, and the arresting policeman (Constable A. Herbert) had to get in the back where the prisoners normally go.

Here's the thing. It's those undignified moments that you will be remembered for. Make one goof and that will achieve immortality. Neil Kinnock falls over on a beach, Ed Miliband attacks a bacon sandwich, and it's constantly resurrected for us to laugh at. When I appeared on *This Is Your Life*, guess which film clip they showed, and who they invited on as a special guest? Constable Herbert. Still, look on the bright side. He revealed that he'd spent many happy dinner parties reminiscing about that achievement. If you can help somebody...

Art Classes

It's fun, and they say neurologically good for your mental acuity, to find a hobby and learn something new at an advanced age. When I used to cruise a lot (in the ocean sense) I loved taking watercolour classes, until I realised that all I was proving to myself was my absence of talent.

So now I have a different hobby: writing to the newspapers. It does frighten me how easily I can adopt the style of Disgusted, Tunbridge Wells. Maybe it's the newspaper etiquette of starting the letter with 'Sir,' which feels like adjusting your monocle or waving your shooting stick. I recommend it as a discipline; expressing a view as cogently as you can, and then seeing it in print, is very satisfying.

Aunts

Aunts, according to tradition, are respectable disciplinarians, conventional, disapproving and the backbone of the family. (Uncles, by contrast, tend to be a bit rascally.)

When the BBC was at its most puritanical and not a rude word was ever heard on the airwaves (remember those distant days?), the broadcaster was always known as Auntie BBC.

I was very fortunate. My grandmother had four daughters, which meant that I grew up surrounded by three highly respectable aunts, who were known as the 'Formidable Leverson Girls'. And they were. Not formidable in the P. G. Wodehouse sense: I never heard 'Aunt calling to Aunt like mastodons over the primeval swamp' as Bertie Wooster did. That was what the telephone was for. My aunts did call to each other: they rang each other every day. They were a tremendous support to each other, the family's bastion instilling respectability in all of us.

An outstanding example of this support was when the oldest sister, Marion, got married. She was 20, and nobody had ever told her the facts of life: not her school, not her nannies, certainly not her mother. So her poor bridegroom had to break the news to her on their honeymoon. She then told her sisters. All four had very happy marriages and children, so it can't have been too traumatic. But it does show that having a close sisterhood can make up for maternal shortcomings.

When aged 14 I had a row with my mother and ran away from home to my grandmother, who gave me meringues for tea and taught me canasta. I spent the night in her comfy spare room and returned home the next day to find my mother furious. 'Your Aunt Nancy was shocked that you burdened your grandmother,' she said. But when I described the evening I had enjoyed, off she went to the phone again to explain to Nancy how spoiled I'd been and how much Granny had enjoyed spoiling me. Not that Nancy was mollified. She was made of sterner stuff.

My aunts surrounded my nuclear family like the ramparts of a castle, very firm but very fair. They remembered everyone's birthdays and upheld family discipline. Once when I was about four years old, I was naughty and my mother sent me to bed without my supper. Totally shocked by such maternal dereliction of duty, I reported her the next day to her oldest sister, my Aunt Marion. She listened and then said, 'Well, Esther, I think that's what happens if you're naughty.' I realised then that the four sisters were a solid phalanx.

In my childhood all the aunts lived within a couple of miles of their mother, my grandmother. That's what an extended family meant: a constant presence in our lives. My cousins were like brothers and sisters; we met and played with each other every weekend. Things have changed so much. Not for the better. My own sister, a terrific aunt to my children, lives in Australia so she's a much more remote presence. Though we do speak to each other every day via the blessed internet, it's not the same. And that has happened all over the country: families are scattered, and children have lost the constant influence of their aunts. No wonder the nation has gone to the dogs.

Baking

(See also *Cake*)

Interestingly, alongside the rise in popularity of cookery shows on TV, especially but not only *The Great British Bake Off*, there has also been a rise in obesity. Just mentioning it, not casting blame. It could be coincidence, I suppose. Although these celebrity chefs do slop huge dollops of butter and sugar into everything, let alone other no-nos such as salt. When compiling their recipes, health never seems to get a look-in with these celebrities. But on the other hand, since home-cooked meals get a far better write-up from nutritionists than ready meals and other highly processed foodstuffs, maybe I shouldn't blame TV cooks entirely for our fatness. Somebody once told me it's the fault of breastfeeding because, this adult male expert told me, breast milk is sweet. Though I don't like to guess how he knew. Maybe he just had a very, very long memory.

I remember that I used to bake as a teenager, loved making puddings and cakes. I once tried to make such an elaborate chocolate cake that even after hours in the oven it was still liquid, so in the end I fried it. Not to be recommended. I do remember how gorgeous a fatless sponge sandwich was, eaten fresh from the oven, filled with raspberry jam and whipped cream. Though it was never so nice the day after. So many things are like that: gorgeous the night before, disappointing in the next morning's light.

Why don't healthy things, like five vegetables a day, have the same seductive power to tempt us? It is quite annoying, when you see a freshly baked scone piled high with clotted cream and jam, that symbolises love and makes us feel cherished in a way that no celery stick or carrot baton ever can. And yet I presume that when the first hominids climbed down from their trees and strode across the prairies of Africa, unless they milked a passing giraffe or squeezed a mango, jam and cream were not part of their diet. So where do we get this addiction to foods that are bad for us?

However it arose, we do need something to strengthen our will to resist. So I strongly recommend that if you are about to watch one of these baking programmes, you fill yourself up with nourishing soup beforehand. Otherwise you will drool all the way through.

Ballet

Call me a philistine, but ballet is profoundly misogynist. I don't think balletomanes and choreographers like women. Look what they ask of them. Not just to point their toes and skip lightly around the stage, oh no. Since around

1830, ballerinas have had to arch their feet and balance *en pointe* with their whole weight on their big toes, which cripples their feet and fills those elegant satin shoes with blood. They even have to jump onto their suffering big toes, which is both precarious and agonising. A horse does it, true enough, but has evolved a nice strong hoof to carry the weight. A famous prima ballerina once said, 'Look for the ballet dancer on the beach, and she'll be the one hiding her damaged toes in the sand.' No wonder.

Male ballet dancers are at least expected to be athletic and strong enough to jump and lift. Soloist prima ballerinas have to be fragile, skinny, submissive to the partners who lift and twirl them, and the *corps de ballet* is regimented to within an inch of its life.

And it's not just physical torment. Talented little girls are weighed and measured so often to keep them thin as stick insects; I wonder how many end up with eating disorders? Have you ever seen a successful ballerina with boobs and a bum? Dancers are crippled by the desire to look artificially 'beautiful', for example to obey the insane need to 'turn out' their hips in a completely unnatural way. It is not surprising that as they grow older they develop back, hip and knee injuries, and the damage often starts when they are very young.

The sad thing is that so few voices are prepared to argue with the accepted opinion of what is 'beautiful'. One of them, Dr Derek Ochiai of the Virginia Sportsmedicine Institute, who is medical consultant for the Washington Ballet, specialises in hip issues. He is quoted in the 2017 report by Romper, a New York-based website about motherhood, as saying 'Ballet ... puts a ton of stress on the hip, forcing external rotation, where you put your legs into positions that 95 percent of the population can't manage.' Cartilage and Achilles tendon tears, hip flexor strains, and foot and ankle issues are common, the report goes on to state, and this harm is not only suffered by professionals. In a year, according to Romper, 'Ochiai has seen at least three dancers, just 15 or 16 years old, with hip injuries so severe they required surgery.'

I recognise there are advantages in being trained in ballet. There is a grace and elegance in the way ballerinas stand and use their arms, although the compulsion to have turned-out hips and feet makes them walk like ducks. But until the medical profession is prepared to fight for the mental and physical health of little girls addicted to the idea of becoming fairy princesses in tutus, the damage will continue to happen, and the training will carry on injuring them (see *Beauty*).

Once I interviewed Dame Margot Fonteyn, for the Radio 4 programme *Start the Week*. She arrived looking regal, and with her light, clipped voice, was quite intimidating. When I asked her if she felt she had sacrificed a normal childhood to her training, she looked haughtily at me, and denied it. Years later it was revealed that as a teenager she had been seduced by the Royal Ballet's founder and music director, Constant Lambert. Hardly surprising that she ended up penniless, having spent the end of her life and her bank account caring for her ruthless husband, Tito Arias. Before she died she once said, 'I can't think why anyone dances. It hurts so much; one's almost always in pain somewhere.'

So until fashions change, and women who ballet dance

are allowed to be curvy and strong, and stay off their own big toes: if your daughter lusts after a gauzy tutu and rosebuds in her hair (or if your son does, for that matter), I would recommend that they enjoy their dreams as much as they want while they are little, but move on to other less dangerous hobbies as they become teenagers. Such as boxing or fire-eating.

Banisters

Install them (see *Falls*). And when walking up or down stairs or steps, cling on to them. Stairs can kill. There are tragic cases of people falling down stairs and fracturing their skulls. So hang on for dear life.

BBC

I'd better declare an interest straight away. I'm not going to be objective about the Beeb, I owe it too much. My father worked for the Beeb for many years, and so did I. Pop was an electrical engineer, and he went to work for the BBC in the thirties, having previously worked for Marconi's. Marconi was a great friend of Mussolini and shared his anti-Semitic views about Jews, so when it became clear that my father was no longer welcome in Marconi's, off he went to join the BBC and Sir John Reith, as he was then.

Speaking about anti-Semitism, Pop was at a very senior meeting at the BBC chaired by Reith (my father always said that people just naturally stood up when Reith came into the room; he was hugely respected) at which someone from the Post Office said something derogatory about Jews. Nobody said anything at the time, but when the meeting ended and Pop went back to his office, a messenger was waiting there asking for him to go back to the DG's office. When he did, Reith made a very fulsome apology to him for the anti-Semitic comment. Pop always admired him for that. You may ask why nobody objected at the time. Good question.

Anyway, because Pop headed up the BBC's Lines and Designs Department (he had overseen the outside broadcast from Windsor Castle when Edward VIII made his abdication speech and worked in Broadcasting House throughout World War II, looking after wireless broadcasts to the Resistance in France), we had one of the first television sets after the war, in 1946. Pop was very keen on quality.

Not the quality of the programme, the engineering quality. He didn't have the highest opinion of television programmes. When I joined a programme team he referred to it as 'the backwash of the entertainment industry'. Which I thought was a metaphor from hairdressing, but as Pop was a keen sailor, I think he meant the rubbish you throw out from the back of a boat. Anyway, it wasn't intended to be complimentary.

Around 1950, Pop was seconded from the Beeb to join the telecommunication department of the United Nations in Lake Success, and we spent two years living on Long Island, New York. When that contract ended we came back to England, and although Pop had been promised his BBC job would be kept open for him, it wasn't.

That was my first experience of the way organisations work. So, piece of advice. If you work for a big company, make sure they need and want you more than you need and want them. Otherwise they will grind you into powder.

Pop was unemployed for six months, a desperate time for the family, but then he was taken on by Standard Telephones and Cables's research department, and for some reason worked with Porton Down where they do a lot of secret defence stuff. He never told me what. But I do know it meant that he was one of the earliest customers of the fabulous hotel and restaurant Chewton Glen, and had many business lunches there. Which they never forgot, so when we had special birthday and Christmas lunches there they made a wonderful fuss of Pop. Including at his 90th birthday party, when Pop said to me, 'This is the happiest day of my life.' So that's something to aim at, isn't it?

Pop never lost his respect for the Beeb, so it was natural for me to apply for a job there straight from university, and they took me on as a sound effects girl, a studio manager in the radio. Although it was quite the wrong job for me, I have some indelible memories.

I started work in Bush House at the World Service. It was full of foreign men, far from home, who preyed upon us studio managers. A friend was bitten by a Brazilian in the lift. I was taken for drinks in the bar of the Hilton. Neither of us much enjoyed either experience.

Once I had to look after the sound of an important broadcast to India. The studio was full of distinguished Indian politicians, and I was alarmed by a deep rumbling sound punctuating their conversation. The building was prone to drilling, and the occasional tube train passing underneath, but finally we in the control room realised it was somebody's stomach.

When I had been a studio manager for only about three weeks, I was booked to put the records on for a listeners' request programme beamed out to Africa. We had to keep exactly to time, because the transmissions were controlled by a computer that switched programmes from country to country precisely to the second.

I was late, so I ran into the studio with an armful of records, hastily introduced myself to the African presenter, tripped and the discs flew out of my hands and down the back of the grams bank, a heavy piece of wooden furniture (called, I think, a TD/7) which was 'lend lease', having been lent to the BBC by America during the war. Twenty years had gone by, but it was still working well in Bush House, though doubtless obsolete everywhere else in the world.

At that moment the programme had to start, so I flicked the presenter's microphone open, knelt on the floor, took a coat hanger and tried to hook the records out from underneath the record player. To my relief the presenter kept talking for the full 15 minutes until the computer clicked us off the air and I got up, not having retrieved a single disc. I brushed myself down, thanked the presenter, and asked what on earth he had found to talk about. He said, 'I told the listeners that my studio manager had only been doing the job for three weeks, she had dropped all the records down the back of the equipment, and now she was on the floor, trying to hook them out with a coat hanger ...' He'd kept his audience entranced for 15 minutes with his commentary on my struggles.

That's when I learned that the world over, people prefer mistakes to programmes.

I did that job for two and a half years, ending up making 'spot' sound effects for radio drama and reaching my high point by playing Juliet in *Romeo and Juliet*, but only after her death, when my body, and hers, fell to the floor. I made a speciality of falling bodies: for another play I had to be an ice-skating accident, and had to fall over five times before the producer was satisfied with the sound of my flesh hitting a wooden plank. I limped up to the office and resigned.

Then I spent six months unemployed and, like my father before me, found it soul-destroying. In fact I spent more and more of each day in bed. Finally I rang a friend I'd met at university, John Spicer: he contacted his mother, who was something important in the Beeb. She interviewed me, hired me as a clerk, and from there I managed to get a job as a researcher for Ned Sherrin, the man who created satire, and David Frost, on television.

The lesson I learned then is one I tell every young person who is frustrated in their job and longs to move on. If you have a string, pull it. Use every contact. There is a logic in this. Interviews are notoriously bad at enabling anyone to assess your skills. They just don't work. I've never got a single job from an interview (you may say that doesn't prove much, but psychologists agree that interviews don't work). It's far better to have a recommendation from someone who has worked with you and knows if you can cut the mustard.

However, since for many people the job interview may be the only way to get through the door, I recommend that you find a friend, or hire a mentor, and practise. A very close friend of mine hired an ex-head teacher who trained her to uncross her arms, flick the hair off her face, lift her chin, make eye contact, and rehearse the best answers to predictable questions. She was encouraged to talk about her real passion and her willingness to go anywhere and do anything for the work required. I watched her confidence visibly grow, and the result was transformational. My friend got the job.

In my case, I met the wonderful Mrs Joanna Spicer, who was Assistant Controller of Domestic Programme Planning (known as ACDPP: one of the Beeb's less exotic sets of initials. They did have an executive whose initials were EIEIO) and she took me on in her department. One happy day I was having a drink with a friend in the BBC Club (now long defunct for health and safety reasons) when I heard that Ned Sherrin was looking for a researcher for his latest series, so I applied. He had staff already on his team who had performed with me in student revues, so they spoke up for me. It was the biggest break of my working life, and I knew it. Lucky me.

Luckier still, all the time I was being trained by the BBC in public service broadcasting. Oh, I know how infuriating the Beeb can be. Of course I do. Above all they are terribly bad at saying goodbye. When they axed my talk show, they never told me, just sent me a manky bunch of flowers with a card saying 'Thanks for the last seven years' and I was expected to deduce that meant goodbye. At the end of 39 years, someone held a farewell party for me on the very day my swipe card ran out so I couldn't get into the building. When they did let me in, a friend looked around the assembled battered buffet and said, 'How interesting, Esther. They've put together all the things you never eat.' But there is something endearing about all that, something Reithian.

But the real delight is the creative freedom, only having to make programmes to entertain, inform and educate the audience. Not the advertisers. Not the shareholders. The audience. Bless you, Beeb, for all your quirks and the mistakes you always over-apologise for. The world would be a duller, more ignorant place without you.

Beauty

What is it? Who decides? Rubens, who delighted in paint-ing rosy exuberant flesh, would have thought the heroin chic of today's fashion models was incredibly ugly. We think his models should be referred to an obesity clinic. Although the Kardashian bum looks as if we are heading back towards Rubens.

Being beautiful gives you power and makes you vulnerable. Especially in an age when each wrinkle is regarded as a disfigurement. The gorgeously evergreen Dame Joan Collins said that the problem with beauty is that it's like being born rich and getting poorer. And she should know. It's interesting, and sad, that two of the greatest beauties of our time, Marilyn Monroe and Princess Diana, both died at the age of 36, at the threshold of middle age. So at the peak of their gorgeousness, and I suppose believing that most of their influence, their power and their wealth depended upon their looks, they were looking forward with dread to years of trying to stave off more and more damage done by time. Dying in their prime means they will never grow old now: their beauty is immortal.

I remember interviewing Eartha Kitt late in her career, the singer once described by Orson Welles as the most exciting woman in the world. I thought her cat-like face was still fascinating, but when I walked past her dressing room I saw her staring at her reflection. I've never forgotten her expression of sheer terror. (The programme also remains engraved in my mind because I had invited my parents to join the studio audience, and afterwards my mother marched up to Eartha Kitt in the hospitality room and said, 'All right then, give us a song.' The moral of that is to never allow your parents in to hospitality, if you mind what they might say).

For those of us who have never experienced what it's like to be beautiful, growing older holds fewer fears. I remember when I passed my driving test first time (pardon the gloat): when I returned to my car and showed my instructor my pass certificate with pride, he said, 'There you are. It's not just the pretty ones.'

As I spent the most sensitive years, from 15 to 25, with an extra layer of what an uncle called my 'puppy fat', I knew that you had to be good company if you wanted to attract friends, and boyfriends. Even when I lost my chubbiness, with my huge teeth and protruding chin only a horse would admire my looks. In my youth I longed to look like my contemporaries, teenage friends who were slender and sexy and could wear the most fashionable clothes, while I was hiding underneath shapeless cardigans. Now, I think I was lucky. I didn't have nearly as much to lose with age.

Beliefs

Why do we believe what we believe? Pro-Brexit, anti-Brexit, religious or anti-religious, whatever you believe: own up, it's a tribal gut reaction. Do we look for evidence and base our views on the facts? Absolutely not. Come election time, we vote with our emotions, not with our intellect. So the politicians will promise us bread and circuses, they tell us they won when they lost, they embark on horrible wars and say we are bound to win because God, or the Party, are on our side, and alas we want to believe them, so we do.

Not just politicians: religions ask us to believe in them. That's what faith means; we believe the wildest promises, like the good go to heaven and the bad go to hell. What can we actually know about what happens after we die? Nothing. Let's face it, Descartes was probably right. All we really know is that 'I think, therefore I am.' Everything else is guesswork.

So you might expect as we grow older that we would admit how much we don't know and stop pretending we

My A–Z of surviving almost everything

are always right. But no. As the years go by, our beliefs get more and more entrenched. And very often our views are based on the belief that our generation got it right and the youth of today are quite wrong. Now there we have a point.

Best Before

Here's a real gulf between the generations. My children scrutinise every sell-by, use-by date on each label, and they ruthlessly turf out anything in their fridge or mine that hangs on past the moment inscribed on the packet or jar. Personally I belong to the scrape-the-mould-off-the-jam school of thought recommended by the then prime minister, Theresa May. Also to my mother's view that if it smells OK and hasn't grown hair, it's perfectly edible. Do I suffer from stomach upsets? Yes, I do, but I try not to mention that to my children or they'll chuck away even more.

Boilers

Have you noticed that they never break down in the summer, when you don't need central heating, and don't rely on hot water so much, but the moment the weather grows chilly, they give up the ghost? There is definitely a conspiracy of machine versus humans. Heaven help us when boilers develop AI. They'll probably decide to spend the winter in Florida and leave you and me behind to freeze.

Bollocks

Is this, or isn't this, a forbidden word? I ask because I have been tripped up by it in the past. When the lovely presenter Susanna Reid was presenting BBC news programmes, I was invited on her breakfast show to be interviewed about reasons why many older people are uncomfortable with the internet. Susanna said that her mother thought it was because new media, emails for instance, are too fast for older people, who can't think that quickly. I took that amiss, and said, 'What's polite for "bollocks"?'

To my surprise Susanna turned to camera and said, 'I would like to apologise to anyone who was offended by something Esther has just said.' I was shocked that she needed to apologise for me and protested, 'But it's an eight-letter word, and just a piece of anatomy.' I was defended by the male co-presenter, who agreed with me – perhaps it being an item of his own anatomy he was proud of. So I went home and looked it up.

Helpfully, in December 2000 a paper was published jointly by the BBC, the Broadcasting Standards Commission, the Advertising Standards Authority and the Independent Television Commission, called 'Delete Expletives'. They collected in it all the rude words they could think of, so I don't recommend reading it if you are of a nervous disposition.

The report was based on a very detailed survey of the public, and 'bollocks' was in the list at number eight: 25 per cent of the people surveyed thought it was quite a strong swear word, but 34 per cent thought it was quite mild. The report stressed that the time of day was important: strong language was tolerated late in the evening, but not first thing in the morning. And of course it depends on who the audience is. Most people try not to swear in front of children in the home. In 2019 an MP used the word in Parliament and was complained about to the Speaker, John Bercow, who ruled it was 'not disorderly'. After the Brexit vote, some Remainers, especially the Liberal Democrats, adopted it as a slogan, with a campaign hat declaring 'Bollocks to Brexit'. They still lost.

So it is clearly controversial and of course times change usage (see *The F Word*). Now that I'm older and wiser, would I use it again at breakfast time on television? No. But Miriam Margolyes wouldn't blench (unless she thought it was too mild for her). But then she has used all kinds of language on breakfast television. So the moral is, I suppose, that if you are tempted to use controversial language – unless you are Miriam – choose your audience with care, and the time of day with even greater care.

Boredom

I wonder if boredom is an affliction of the young? I once helped to make a television programme about growing older, called *Never Too Late*, and one of the striking results of a survey of older people's attitudes was that they told us they were never bored. One of them explained why: she said she had 'too much mental furniture'. I have a friend, whom I have never met but who is one of the callers to The Silver Line (see *The Silver Line*), who has agoraphobia and literally never leaves her home. I asked what she does there day after day, and she told me, 'I have my memories.' Both of them had so many thoughts, ideas and memories that it never occurred to them to be bored.

I realise that this is not always true. Another Silver Line friend of mine is very physically disabled, but mentally extremely active. She remembers a time not all that long ago when she went dancing, met friends, really enjoyed her life, and now feels imprisoned. So the Silver Line friends, who ring her every week, and her daughters, make her life worth living. It's not that she's bored. She's incredibly frustrated: her body just refuses to keep up with her mind.

Learning new things is the perfect way to stave off boredom. Television does help, especially the antiques shows and the quizzes much watched and enjoyed by older viewers, but which have been lambasted by a BBC news chief for wasting airtime. The point of these programmes is that you can learn all kinds of things from watching them, and that's the other unremarked aspect of growing older: you definitely want to keep on learning.

And giving yourself time to reflect. Until the Covid-19 pandemic struck, I had no time for reflection. I was buzzing around like a manic wasp, from meeting to meeting, event to event, never allowing myself time to wonder whether I was actually making any difference, and if I could or should be spending more time with my much-loved family and friends.

By great good luck, in the spring of 2020 just before the Covid lockdown hit, I was working in a holiday cottage we've owned for years in the beautiful New Forest in Hampshire. Hearing the rumours of an imminent pandemic, I dashed up the motorway to my flat in London and back again, grabbing some changes of underwear just in case a lockdown was imposed for longer than a week. I've lived in the Forest ever since. Having been a Londoner for almost eighty years, I even sold my London flat without ever going back to it again.

Do you remember that spring in 2020? March in the New Forest was like Paradise: golden shafts of sunlight, soft sweet air, trees just coming into bud, and for the first time I could watch the seasons change, day by day.

Was I bored? Not for a moment. Perhaps it is because I realise that my time is limited. Unlike the bored teenager, I can't look forward to year after year, stretching like the Gobi Desert into the distance. I know that, like it or not, I will fall off my perch some time fairly soon, so I must appreciate and treasure every moment I'm given. And I do. Savouring life, in a kind of granular way that I had no idea was possible when I was younger and was constantly impatient for the next adventure.

Not, of course, that I blame the young. Without their impatience, their ambition, their courage and risk-taking, humanity would still believe the world was flat and the wheel would never work. But the price of their lust for adventure is that when nothing appears to be happening, the same old fire is flickering in the grate, or the same old rose is blooming on the thorn, they get terribly bored. Whereas we oldies stare into the flames, or sniff the rose, and think how lucky we are.

Which may be why the young have had to invent and learn mindfulness. Don't tell them, but we oldies do it effortlessly all the time.

Boxing

The reason many young people take up boxing is because every other way to excel, to make money or to defeat prejudice has been denied to them. It is noticeable how many champion boxers have come from minority communities. Of course boxing demands outstanding courage, talent and skill. But that doesn't mean it's a noble sport. The point of boxing is to hurt your opponent, and hopefully knock him/her out. Look at the glorious Muhammad Ali, reduced to a shadow by the punishment his head took over the years. Do we really want our sons, or our daughters, to be trained to inflict such injury? Is it really liberation for women to take up boxing? For that matter, is it liberation for women to be trained as soldiers in the front line, to kill or maim the enemy? Haven't women too much sense? It appears not.

Breastfeeding

I have been brought up to believe that breastfeeding is a mother's duty. My grandmother did it, but family legend says that she was so horrified by the process that she hid herself under a large shawl: face, chest, everything, while it went on. My mother did it. And I did it, and it hurt like hell.

I gather it doesn't hurt everyone, but my theory is that those lovely classical pictures of the Madonna and child doing it should show her flinching and screwing up her face in pain. It got less painful as time went by, so after a year or so I could multitask. I have actually driven while breastfeeding, unable to stand the baby passenger crying lustily from hunger. That was around forty years ago, so I hope the statute of limitations has kicked in and I cannot now be prosecuted for dangerous driving. Or careless breastfeeding.

My most egregious multitasked breastfeeding was when my second daughter was a baby and came with me to BBC's Broadcasting House, where I was to be interviewed by Gloria Hunniford. While we were waiting in the studio and Gloria was introducing a record, Rebecca began to squirm, which I knew was a warning sign, so I stuck my boob in her mouth and she began contentedly and noisily sucking. Gloria was a bit alarmed at the noise, and apologised to her listeners, telling them that I was in the studio. I protested that the listeners might assume that the sound was me sucking my teeth and explained it was my baby having lunch. Terry Wogan was listening while driving and told me he had to park because he was laughing so much, and later teased Gloria mercilessly.

The weird thing is the way that biology takes over. There is no way on earth I would disrobe to my upper torso in a BBC studio without a hungry baby overriding my inhibitions. Which shows that, civilised as we may think ourselves to be, instinct always wins. And proves yet again that women are expert at multitasking. Can you imagine a man being able to drive or broadcast and breastfeed at the same time?

Bulges

Some bulges are more acceptable than others. Bulging boobs are considered so desirable that cosmetic surgeons make a fortune inserting plastic bits inside to make them bulge even more. Bulging bums are now fashionable too, so some people pay for implants there as well. But bulging stomachs, not so much. So a whole range of underwear has been invented to strap unwanted bulges in. In my teens I used to wear a girdle. It had a double effect, being made of tight elastic material. It held in the tummy bulge, and also acted as a chastity belt.

It was at least slightly more compassionate than the corsets I helped my grandmother to do up, with tough strings lacing rows of whalebone hooks together at the back. She made me pull them as tightly as *Gone With The Wind*'s Scarlett O'Hara had, to emphasise her wasp waist before a party. It looked very uncomfortable.

Nowadays, according to my daughters, there are Spanx and a whole variety of other thigh squashers, bum compressors, and tummy squeezers. For men and women. They can't be good for us. So my view is that if you, like me, have a muffin top bulging over the top of your jeans, learn to love it. There's nothing more delectable on a cold day than a warm muffin.

Cake

Lemon drizzle. Coffee walnut. Victoria sponge filled with jam and cream. The very words are like a song. One day I vow I will bake a cake again, as I used to in my teens (see *Baking*), because the truth is, no shop-bought cake can compare with such warm-from-the-oven, sprinkled-with-caster-sugar, lighter-than-air loveliness. Worth every filling in your teeth, every pound on your scales.

Camilla and Charles

Welcome to the throne. King Charles has earned his place there by being right so often, about conservation, about offering young people support and opportunities, about architecture and the King James Bible. Queen Camilla has earned it by staying silent and surviving all the brickbats, when the world derided her looks and blamed her for the divorce and death of Diana. She is now supporting important neglected causes, such as literacy, domestic abuse and loneliness. Well done Camilla.

Clearly as husband and wife they support each other and supply each other's needs. Good news for them. And Charles has, after all, demonstrated taste and intellect not common in monarchs.

Remember how hideous modern architecture was when he made a speech pointing out that a proposed extension to the National Gallery in London's Trafalgar Square was as ugly as 'a monstrous carbuncle on the face of a much-loved and elegant friend'. The extension was cancelled, but even better, in spite of the rage of the architects who were designing the carbuncles for everyone else to live and work in, and then went home to their own Georgian homes in the countryside, he gave voice to us who were doomed to live among the monstrosities of concrete and glass.

And we need his voice, don't we, to continue to inspire us to protect the planet. I was amused when the *Guardian* moved heaven and earth, taking ten years and spending almost half a million pounds, to expose the fact that Charles had written his notorious 'black spider memos' to various government ministers, and when we read them most were espousing causes which were beyond reproach. Except alternative medicine and homeopathy, but we all have our quirks. Even monarchs. Especially monarchs.

Cars

Dinosaurs ruled the earth for many millions of years, but then a catastrophe, perhaps an asteroid, blasted them into extinction. So because I always get mixed up between the Cretaceous and the Jurassic and all the other geological

Latin names, I just call that whole period the age of the dinosaur. Now that we live with other monsters which look as if they too will become extinct, thanks to the catastrophe of climate change due to fossil fuels like petrol and diesel, perhaps future generations will label our own time as 'the age of the car'. And hopefully before too long cars will also be extinct, only preserved and gawped at in museums.

Other killers, cigarettes for instance, will soon hopefully also become extinct, because no future generation will understand why we set fire to leaves in our mouths, creating horrible diseases and disabilities. And I speak as an ex-smoker so I have all the fervour of a convert and have been known to snatch cigarettes out of young people's mouths. And smoking is indeed becoming unacceptable.

Killer cars, on the other hand, are these days loved and admired more than ever as status symbols, have TV programmes devoted to them, and flamboyant shows and enormously opulent international races built around them. But I suspect that future generations will be just as perplexed by the way we have allowed cars to dominate our lives and our planet. And they kill so many of us: at the last count cars kill well over a million people a year worldwide.

Although my grandmother owned a very early car, and I'm distantly related to the Bentley Boys who used to race around in theirs, I've never much liked cars. When I was in my late teens, in pre-breathalyser, pre-seatbelt days I used to be driven home by drunk young men who boasted, 'I always drive better with a drink inside me', whereas I was sober and saw that they didn't. So I've never warmed to these machines.

Obviously they are extremely useful. Provided they start reliably and their brakes and steering work, they can provide us with a crucial independence. I know the devastating impact on older people when they have their driving licences removed, so I don't underestimate the value of the car taking us from place to place. But all the same, when you look at the damage roads have done to our towns and villages by slicing across the countryside, and the pollution cars cause to the air in our cities, alongside all the people who are killed and injured by them, you have to ask: surely there must be some other way of getting about?

I once heard Rowan Atkinson giving a lecture about his McLaren F1. An engineer himself, he talked lovingly about his car's precision engineering, the gold tools and titanium panels, the fact that you have to be deemed worthy before they will sell you one. But I do recall reading about an accident when he wrapped his around a tree. Also, I asked him if he had ever pranged his when it was new and he told me that when he first drove it to a friend to show it to them, reversing out of the drive he misunderstood his friend's gestures and hit a post. The tiniest dent takes a small fortune to repair. But when he sold it he made a huge profit, so well done, Mr Bean.

But his car would have been wasted on me. I do have friends and family who love cars and are thrilled when they drive around in something expensive and status-worthy. To my interest, when I ask why, they mention boys' toys, the gadgets on the dashboard and the growling noise of the exhaust, so all the stuff they go on about on *Top Gear* about roadholding and how fast they go from nought to sixty seems not to register on the petrolheads in my family.

If and when the energy sources run out, maybe cars will be extinct and we'll fly around in tiny solar-powered air buses, and look back at the age of the car with pity. Until then, I'll just pop to the shops with my little much-pranged runaround, not loving it, but being quite grateful to it, and trying to make sure I don't add to those awful accident statistics.

Cats

Once upon a time when I was working on the BBC consumer programme *That's Life!*, a colleague came into a production meeting carrying a black bin bag. And slowly, before our marvelling eyes, she brought out of it Mimi the cat. That wasn't as cruel as it sounds because Mimi had died some time before. And Elsie, her devoted owner, had loved her so much that when Mimi passed away she decided to immortalise her; found a taxidermist in her local directory and he did his best to stuff her. Mimi, that is.

Or maybe he did his worst. Because although in life Mimi had been a gorgeous white Persian with silky fur and big green eyes, stuffed she looked like a moggie who'd had a wild night on the tiles. Her eyes were crossed, her fur was tufty, her legs were akimbo and she made the team laugh until we cried. All except our boss, programme editor John Morrell, who was horrified that we had the bad taste to laugh at a deceased cat. But he was outvoted, and Mimi was revealed on the show to louder, longer laughs than I have ever heard from a studio audience. In fact the wonderful Les Dawson told me that Mimi was the funni-est thing he had ever seen on television. But our editor John was right, too, because Mimi's item provoked more complaints than anything else on the BBC that weekend, and I was summoned to appear on *Open Air*, the viewers' complaints programme, to defend myself.

I have a guilty conscience about the way I behaved.

First of all they showed the item, with Mimi appearing out of a black rubbish bag and the audience roaring with laughter at her, and then they let Mrs Viewer have her say. 'Miss Rantzen, that was a terrible thing to do to that poor cat, to hold her up to ridicule.'

Now here's the confession. For the first and only time in my career, I lied on camera. I looked deep into the camera with all the sincerity I could muster and answered, 'Mrs Viewer, if you think for one moment we thought the audience would laugh at Mimi, of course we would never have done it.'

Mrs Viewer saw through that at once. 'Don't give me that, Miss Rantzen. I heard you say "that's let the cat out of the bag".'

'Oh dear,' I said. 'That must have been nerves. And in any case,' I said, clutching at straws, 'it was a serious consumer item, because Mimi's owner could sue the taxidermist under the Sale of Goods and Services Act, and if she won he'd be fined.'

Mrs Viewer snorted. 'Fined? Nothing's bad enough for that man. He should be stuffed himself.'

'Let me get this straight,' I said. 'You think laughing at a cat who had passed on some time ago to the great mouse pastures in the sky is terrible, but killing and stuffing the taxidermist is fine?'

'Yes,' said Mrs Viewer, adamantly. 'Nothing's bad enough for that man.'

Which of course doesn't surprise any of us who long ago realised that we British prefer animals to people. Especially cats.

So I hope I won't get into still more trouble if I admit that personally, I have never liked cats (see *Dogs*). Cats are natural killers. I once watched a cat (my late husband loved them, so we had one) leap into the air, claws outstretched, and bring down a robin in flight. But my neighbours had a couple of cats they left behind when they moved to a new house on a main road. They decided that to take a cat there would be dangerous, so allowing them to stay in the home they knew would be kinder to their cats.

But the new neighbours had moved in with a bouncy dog, and the cats took umbrage. One of them, Coco, arrived at my door, skinny and starving. We fed her and found her a good home. Then her brother Boots appeared, equally skinny. He was black with white paws and whiskers and a white tummy: I believe they're called tuxedo cats. We fed him.

He was quite picky, so my daughter found an online cat delicatessen that sends frozen turkey, duck, lamb and beef and he scoffed it down, especially if we added M&S's finest sliced roast chicken breast. We bought a little house for him to shelter in when the weather was inclement. He spurned it. So we took my favourite tuffet from the sitting room, spread a soft blanket on the top, put it into the kitchen and that became his throne. And from then on we had no more trouble with the mice that had plagued us until Boots arrived. Although three times Boots has looked for me in the garden to present me with a dead mouse, or perhaps vole. So now we have doubled our chicken order, cancelled all our holidays, and Boots rules.

I recommend never attempting a tussle of wills with a cat. I mentioned that in a letter to the *Sunday Telegraph* and provoked a lively correspondence from people who pointed out that dogs have owners but cats have servants.

Childcare

Like many of my generation, my mum was a full-time wife and mother. My father was the family's hunter-gatherer, who went out to work to pay for food and shelter. And my sister and I had no doubt that we were our parents' priority, that their children came first. That was the convention, the way society managed childcare. In my extended family, like most others, the women were responsible for the children and supported one another emotionally and practically, while their husbands supported them financially. Old-fashioned as that sounds now, as a division of labour it worked.

My A–Z of surviving almost everything

Today, of course, nobody would put up with women being denied the opportunity to forge careers of their own, instead being expected to become stay-at-home wives and mothers. In any case, successive governments have decided that the only way to prevent child poverty is for both parents to work. Which begs the question, who has time for that most crucial task of all, childcare?

One answer is the army of unpaid, undervalued child carers, the grandparents. Every grandparent I know is actively involved in grandchild-care. They drop their grandchildren off to school and pick them up when both parents are working. They help out with chores and assist financially if they can. Sometimes they become a refuge for grandchildren whose homes and families are unsafe (see *Grandchildren*).

Then there are the paid child carers, the childminders, the day nurseries, the crèches, most so expensive that the fees they cost wipe out the wages Mum and Dad are earning, which makes the whole sacrifice the family is making pointless. Which is also why so many parents can only afford to work part-time, if at all.

And when things go wrong at home, there is the lifeline created by foster parents. I have a friend who grew up in a dangerous home where there was every kind of abuse and neglect. As a child he suffered sexual abuse, physical abuse, emotional abuse and was given so little food that he used to spread toothpaste on pieces of paper to remind him what food tasted like. When Childline launched, he realised that it would provide him, for the first time, with a way to ask for help safely, so he rang the helpline from his school and the Childline volunteer persuaded him to talk to a teacher, with the result that he was taken into foster care. When I met him, he was 40. He had just changed his surname to his foster parents' name, and asked permission to call his foster mother 'Mum', to which she readily agreed. He has created an agency to recruit more foster parents. Foster parents save lives.

The way I managed to wobble across the tightrope stretching between work and the care of my own children was to employ nannies. I was lucky to have a television fat cat's salary, so the nannies did the chores, I did the treats. Did that work? According to my children, who are now grown up, yes and no. The treats were fabulous: holidays, parties, trips to the theatre. And we are all extremely close and protective of each other. But I admit that there were times when I was hunched over a hot typewriter or computer, fighting with a deadline and oblivious to requests from my nearest and dearest, so I do feel guilty that sometimes I was concentrating too hard on my work. So when I say childcare is the most crucial task of all, do as I say, not as I did. And good luck.

Childline

Childline was launched on 30 October 1986, from a tiny London office donated by BT in the shadow of St Paul's Cathedral, in a special programme on BBC1 called *Childwatch*. I didn't realise it at the time, but it brought about a revolution in child protection. And yet it seemed such a simple idea: offering children the possibility of safely seeking help themselves.

The public instantly understood the crucial importance of a helpline for children. So did the children themselves – there were 50,000 attempted calls that first night. The charity had important supporters from the start, from Mrs Thatcher, the prime minister, to BT, who gave it their engineering test number because it was simple enough for a child to remember: 0800 1111, the only phone number which has remained unchanged ever since. And from the beginning, children turned to Childline.

The *Childwatch* programme changed many things, among them the way abused children were treated by the courts and the public's understanding of child abuse. And it also changed my life.

I had already helped to make a landmark programme about drug abuse with presenter Nick Ross and a brilliant production team. *Drugwatch* had been Michael Grade's idea: he had come to run BBC1 from the States, where drug abuse was already a huge problem, and he knew it was only a matter of time before drugs caused the same devastation in Britain. *Drugwatch* was a landmark programme on Sunday night, helping to set up a network of support groups for addicts and their families, so after it went out the BBC asked if I had an idea for another landmark programme.

There had recently been one of those tragic stories that seem to hit the headlines every three or four years, when an abused child's body had been found too late to save her life. Reading the agonising details, I felt that this tragedy could have been preventable. I suggested to the team that we could make a big programme about child protection, in which we could explore better ways of supporting children and saving lives. Michael Grade agreed.

Ritchie Cogan, the *Childwatch* producer, suggested that (as we had done in our *Drugwatch* programme) we could base the programme on a survey of *That's Life!* viewers who had experienced abuse themselves and would be prepared, confidentially, to describe their lives to us. That way we might be able to detect patterns, to guide us to save more children's lives in the future. It turned out to be the biggest survey of its kind.

When we launched the survey on an edition of *That's Life!* and explained its purpose, because we knew so many children watched *That's Life!* we realised that some might be experiencing abuse at that time. So we opened a help-line for children after the programme. The social workers who oversaw it met me on the Monday morning after the programme and told me that the lines had been jammed with children talking for the first time about the abuse they were suffering.

I will never forget that moment, listening to the social workers as we sat together in a shabby office in the BBC; my sudden realisation that this was the most important thing I had ever been involved with, protecting children from avoidable pain. The helplines were only open for 48 hours. Over the two days, around a hundred children rang disclosing abuse they had never dared talk about before. The social workers explained to me that being able to talk about their lives safely for the first time, and being reassured that the abuse or neglect was not their fault, gave the children confidence and hope. I felt sure that thousands more would have wanted to contact the helpline if only it had stayed open. So I suggested to *Childwatch* producer Sarah Caplin that maybe someone should create a special helpline for children, free, and open 24/7.

Sarah wouldn't let me forget the thought (and she became one of the trustees of Childline, supporting the charity for 17 years). She called a meeting of child protection experts, and we told them the results of our survey: that only a tiny minority of the adults who had been abused as children reported that they had any help at all, and most of those said that the help had either made no difference or made things worse.

The experts were not surprised. We asked if any of their charities could create a helpline for children. The experts said no. They all agreed that children would use one, but that it would be impossible to set one up. We went selectively deaf and agreed after the meeting that if they wouldn't create a children's helpline, we would.

Sarah went to discuss our idea with the Department of Health and they advised her to create an independent charity, with a board of trustees and a chair. She, the producer Ritchie Cogan, Ian Skipper and I became trustees, with me as chair.

I had first met Ian Skipper on *That's Life!* when we had told the story of Ben Hardwick, a little boy who was dying of liver disease and urgently needed a liver transplant. Ian had rung the BBC and said, 'Whatever that boy needs, he must have.' He had suggested flying Ben to the States. But Professor Sir Roy Calne was ready to operate on him in Addenbrooke's Hospital in Cambridge, if a donor could be found. As a result of the programme a donor was found, and Ben lived for another year. Ian Skipper became a trustee and supporter of the Ben Hardwick Memorial Fund, which paid for an intensive care bed for children having transplants in Addenbrooke's.

When in 1986 we had the idea of a children's helpline, I remember having lunch with Ian and explaining to him why it was so necessary. He asked how much cash we would need. I said half a million to cover the overheads before the fundraising kicked in. He said, 'I think we can do that.' Ian was like that, a genuine philanthropist. He helped us create the Childline charity (Sarah invented the name) and was a trustee until his death.

When the *That's Life!* survey came in, the results were heart-stopping. I remember one woman reporting: 'I was never frightened of going home from school alone in the dark, of being raped or mugged, because I knew what was waiting for me at home was far worse than that could ever be.' Another told us that, unable to bear what her mother and mother's partner were doing to her, when a teacher she trusted asked the class to write an essay from her own life, she described the abuse. She waited eagerly for the teacher to read it. When the essays were returned, hers was thrown on the desk in front of her with a red line through it, and the comment: 'Never let me read such a disgusting invention again.' She never dared ask for help again.

The *That's Life!* helpline taught me an important lesson. I had assumed that the children would use it to seek help, and that our role would be to contact the police or the social services on the children's behalf. I was wrong. Abused children were extremely reluctant to identify themselves: they had been threatened into silence, they feared asking for help would bring disaster upon them, they had to be persuaded that they had the right to safety and that things could change for the better.

As our survey had found, all too often trying to bring in help only made things worse for them. The social workers in charge of the *That's Life!* helpline told me of one little girl who had rung to report that her father was sexually abusing her. At my urging they persuaded her to disclose her name and address and sent a police officer round. When he arrived, the father opened the front door with his arm around the silent child, and when the officer revealed why he had been called, the father laughed and said, 'She's got such a sense of humour, she must have seen something on television and decided to have a joke.' And he shut the door, leaving the child in even greater danger.

I learned that if an abuser knows a child has disclosed abuse, they will use any method to silence the child. I know of a child whose leg was broken to keep him silent; children have been threatened with Mum or Dad going to prison, the puppy being drowned, and of course that they will not be believed. So in Childline, unless a child's life is in immediate danger, we do not break a child's confidentiality. We work at the child's pace, to ensure a child is never intimidated into retracting and then placed in even greater peril.

I also learned that the vast majority of abusers are within the child's family or circle of friends, and that creates a terrible paradox for the child. Often they love the abuser, but they hate the abuse. In Childline's earliest days I took a phone call from a child who told me how much she hated the pornographic photographs she was forced to take part in by her father and his friends. She was ringing not to protect herself, but her little six-year-old sister he was now threatening to include. I said she must tell me where she was, so that she and her sister could be protected. She said, 'No, because if I do you will come and take monster Daddy away, and then I'll lose lovely Daddy as well.' Like so many abused children, she wanted to stop the abuse, but not to lose the family she loved.

After Fred and Rosemary West, the serial killers, had been convicted for their terrible crimes, I heard that their children had talked about ringing Childline so that they could protect their oldest sister, Heather, from being abused (and in the end murdered). They decided that they didn't dare because if anyone knew the crimes that were being committed in their home, they would lose the only thing they had: each other. And that did indeed happen.

Looking back over the years since Childline launched, there have been so many challenges, but wonderful moments too. Diana, the Princess of Wales, immediately supported Childline with a personal donation, and opened our new bases in London and Scotland (see *Diana*). Just before she died, she launched our Tenth Birthday Appeal in the Savoy Hotel, and wrote a foreword for our Christmas book. Margaret Thatcher gave us a reception in Number 10, putting us on the map with government ministers and with donors, as did John Major. Gordon Brown gave us a grant which enabled us to launch our online service. Sophie, the Countess of Wessex, became our patron, and then became patron of the whole NSPCC when we merged with that great charity.

Alongside the great and the good who supported us were all the people who ran for Childline, slimmed for Childline, made cookies for Childline, and raised the funds we needed to help more than five million children. Soon after Childline launched, I opened a brown envelope with a gold wedding ring inside it. The letter explained it was all the owner possessed of value – she was a widow and she wanted us to sell it to pay for the calls from children. That commitment was then, and is now, a constant inspiration. But the most inspiring moments of all are when someone tells me of the invaluable support they received from Childline when they were children and had nowhere else to turn.

Over the years, the service has changed in ways we could never have predicted. Beside the phone line we now have online counselling, message boards and emails, all equally child-centred and sensitive. As time has gone by, I have now met so many adults who have explained that without Childline they would not be here today. And from their stories I have discovered what I describe as 'the upward spiral'.

Experts sometimes discuss the 'downward spiral' of abuse infecting generation after generation. But nobody seems to have noticed that it works the other way, that if you help and protect children in an effective and timely way, they never forget it and they are determined to give back.

When I wrote *Running Out of Tears*, a book of profiles of a dozen young adults who had rung Childline as abused children, they unanimously told me that Childline had transformed their lives. A Childline counsellor had assured them that the abuse was not their fault, that things could change for the better, and that gave them confidence and hope. Hope is what makes life worth living. And those dozen children grew up to become a nurse, the founder of a charity, a social worker, a therapist working in prisons, two fundraisers, a teacher: every single one was giving back the help they had received. The upward spiral in action.

Childline consists of staff and volunteers who put children first, day in, day out. I have learned over the years I have worked alongside them that no matter how gloomy the day's news is, however dark life may seem, we must remember all these people all over the world who represent the good, the positive, who put other people first and who give us all hope.

Cleaning

Some people can dance, some can sing or paint, some can clean. It's an amazing talent. Like Mary Poppins clicking her fingers and making everything fly into cupboards and drawers, talented cleaners can bring shining order to the grimiest, most rubbish-strewn room. Not that you or I live in such disorder, but there is an aspect of chaos theory which means that day by day things seem to have a life of their own, accreting in nooks and crannies and invading our space unless a talented cleaner whips them into shape.

Personally, I have the opposite talent. I can clean a room thoroughly and it will end up looking even less appetising. I watch the cleaning experts avidly on television programmes which have names like *The World's Worst Hoarder* and *How Can Anyone Live Like This?* and try to learn from them, but it never seems to increase my skill. It just makes me feel even more inadequate.

We did do occasional cleaning items on *That's Life!*, but all that taught me was that you can clean copper saucepans with ketchup, which makes me wonder what ketchup does to our intestines. So my conclusion is to never underestimate the wonder of natural-born cleaners; nurture them and, if you are rich enough, delegate your cleaning to them. They are worth it.

Collagen

A doctor once told me that using face creams that contain collagen to try and eradicate wrinkles is about as sensible as sticking a steak to your face. It can't get into the skin to do any good, so don't bother. Which makes sense because if you could do that, why would anyone go to the time, expense and put themselves through the pain of facelifts and fillers?

Colours

A normally chic female colleague of mine walked into the office one morning wearing a new outfit in a lurid shade of mustard yellow. She explained that she had undergone 'colour analysis'. This consists of some kind of mumbo jumbo where you visit a 'colour expert' about 'warm colours' and 'cold colours', and whether you are winter or summer. I admit I drifted a bit while she explained it. She then revealed that she also had an outfit in cyclamen pink. I shared with her my view that the two colours to avoid at all costs, whether you are 'summer' or 'winter', are mustard yellow and cyclamen pink. The most flattering colours are soft pastels, like coral and aquamarine. Black only works on the young. White reflects flatteringly up onto a mature face, hence pearls. Grey is a bit depressing. Beige is beige.

However, who am I to judge? As Victoria Wood once said about my taste in clothes, 'I don't know why people go on about her teeth, have you seen her dresses?' (see *Victoria Wood*).

Company

The antidote to loneliness. As long as it's congenial company, otherwise you're better on your own. But finding excellent companions is not easy: it can take a lifetime to identify them and make them yours. So here are my personal criteria. It doesn't matter if you don't vote the same way, or enjoy the same food, or appreciate the same books, plays, films or programmes: you must laugh at the same things. And, sadly, you probably need roughly the same disposable income, otherwise envy can get in the way.

Complaining

There are two ways to complain: be nice, or be horrible. Both have their strengths.

- Be nice. Whether it's on the phone or by email, the secret is that you are extraordinarily nice but you make sure that you escalate your charmingly phrased complaint as far up as you can go. You describe how greatly you value them, their work, their mission, and explain that you are as deeply distressed as they, their CEO, their chair, their investors, the press will be to know how badly they have let you down. You explain the damage they have done you, and all those who depend upon you. And you copy your email, or you duplicate your phone call to every senior executive in the company you can identify, especially in their communications department.

- Be horrible. This works with builders, or carpet layers, who are letting everyone down and therefore move to the top of the list anyone who chews their ears off until they do. But otherwise it's risky. At best they will just hang up. At worst you will receive packets of something nasty through the letter box.

Confidence

If you were Sleeping Beauty, and I was your fairy godmother, the one gift I would give you – forget the handsome prince to kiss you awake, that's too contentious what with issues of consent etc. – would be confidence. Ask any performer, any politician, any writer, any athlete, and they will tell you that confidence means having enough self-belief to get a standing ovation, to win an election, to write a bestseller and to set a world record.

By which I don't mean the overblown Trumpian confidence, which means he can say anything and he thinks everyone will believe his crazy 'alternative facts' (and tragically, far too often far too many do). What I mean is having the confidence not to be intimidated but to be liberated to do your best. So where does the right kind of confidence come from?

It could be nature, it could be nurture; it's probably a combination of both. Praising children can raise their feelings of self-worth. But so can setting them high standards. A happy marriage or partnership can pick you up when you feel down. Just as a bad one can undermine and gaslight us into blaming ourselves for any perceived failure, and into feeling worthless. Some of us have more resilience, some have less. Who knows why?

Confidence can be built up, but it can also be eroded, we do know that. The experience of many of today's young people who contact Childline is that social media do not help boost their self-worth. They find themselves competing with other young people for likes, for success, for good looks, and they're spending more and more of their lives communing with the unreal world of their screens and tablets, driving themselves into feeling lonelier and less popular than all their friends.

But the good news is that for many older people, confidence grows with experience and age. People who were unsure of themselves as teenagers – and what teenager has not felt unsure at some stage? – gradually reassure themselves as they discover that other people aren't much more competent, or sexy, or clever than they are. And if we are lucky enough to find a role, or a job, where we can learn a skill and reach the point where we really know what we are doing, that is a terrific boost. Ageism of course has the opposite effect, and makes some older people feel that they are long past their sell-by date. One early caller to The Silver Line said that when he put the phone down at the end of a conversation, he felt as if he'd joined the human race. He should have always felt that he was a highly valued member of humanity, especially as he grew older.

I had a great-aunt who was a Christian Scientist, so she used to take her medicines with her eyes shut, or so the family mythology claimed. But she also used the Coué method of self-healing, looking at herself in the mirror every morning and telling herself, 'Every day in every way I am getting better and better.' Not a bad philosophy applied to old age. By the time we're all a hundred, we'll know that we're perfect. There's confidence for you.

Cosmetic Surgery

The great taboo topic. Isn't it a coincidence that all those television presenters with square faces, blank foreheads and pouting lips owe that to Pilates and bottled water? I once appeared in a programme with the great film actress Shelley Winters. She sat down in the make-up room and said to the make-up artist, 'No surgeon has ever touched my face.' She must have been in her late sixties at the time. Then she took out a small box, and produced two little golden hooks, a couple of shoelaces and some glue. The make-up artist carefully glued the hooks to her cheeks, threaded the laces through them, yanked them up as hard as she could and tied them in a knot on the top of her head. Shelley's face moved up a good three inches. Then a wig covered the lot.

The trouble with cosmetic surgery is that it can become addictive. Don't start unless you are extremely tolerant of hospitals, have the time and have the funds. Colleagues of mine seem to have procedures at least every year. The sad thing is that there was a time when older faces were considered beautiful without hooks or laces. See Whistler's mother, for instance. These days she would look like Whistler's daughter.

Covid

What an ordeal the world has suffered, the pandemic created by an extraordinary new virus, especially targeting the old. What a terrible martyrdom that courageous Chinese ophthalmologist, Dr Li Wenliang, suffered, who first identified how dangerous Covid was and who was then forced by the Wuhan police to recant, and eventually died from the virus aged 33. Now he has become a hero revered around the world, small consolation for his widow and their two little children. How many lives could have been saved had he been believed from the first? Not for the first time a lynch mob (in this case state sponsored, the police who hauled him in and have now apologised, too late) has proved murderous and self-destructive. But in the darkness we must remember that throughout the pandemic there have been stories like his, of extraordinary unselfishness and dedication.

But we must learn from the failures. We cannot use ignorance as an excuse for our mistakes. Some politicians like to remind us that Covid was unknown before late 2019. And yet one hundred years before, my great-aunt Lizzy's 18-year-old daughter died in a different, even more lethal, pandemic: the Spanish flu. She was one of a quarter of a million deaths, most of young healthy people, who died in the UK. There were more deaths worldwide from Spanish flu than happened throughout World War I. So millions of families know only too well the personal tragedies that the statistics represent. When Covid struck we were unprepared for a pandemic, and probably still are. The overriding lesson we must learn is that we live in a multi-connected world; we cannot isolate or insulate ourselves against our neighbours. If an infectious disease strikes, the whole world is at risk.

Critics

Did you know that Bizet died of a heart attack at the age of 36 after the scathing critical reviews of his last opera? Guess which one. Yes, *Carmen*, the most performed and most deeply loved opera of all. Just mentioning it. So no matter how deeply you are insulted by professional critics or amateurs, the trick is – unlike Bizet – don't let the bastards grind you down. Think how many more fabulous operas we would be enjoying now if the critics had been less abusive and Bizet had been more resilient. (Yes, I know I said I don't enjoy opera, but don't expect me to be consistent. And everybody loves *Carmen*.)

Cruising

If you don't possess your own private yacht, which always seems to me to be rather vulgar, cruising is a great substitute (in the ocean sense). Unpack once, and someone else will do the steering so you wake up somewhere different to explore or not, as you choose. And en route you are surrounded with scenes of incredible beauty: wonderful sunsets, dolphins, whales, the most gorgeous seascapes. And if you like dressing up, rattling your jewellery, learning ballroom dancing or watercolours, you can fill every waking hour. Especially eating and drinking – the food never stops.

However, it is my duty also to point out the downsides. If there is only one laundry room, it has been known for fisticuffs to break out when somebody nicks someone else's tumble dryer.

Bad weather can cause acute nausea, especially for the richest passengers in top-floor suites – a form of redistribution. Usually the ship's doctor will have anti-sickness tablets or injections that work well and quickly.

I prefer small ships, even though they do rock around a bit more. Very large ships overwhelm little ports and can't get into lovely villages. But beware of paying for too many onshore excursions. Coach trips can be guided by interminable bores. Bear in mind the Rantzen Rule of tourism: you'll only ever remember three facts about anywhere you visit, and you can usually find those in a guidebook. So when you arrive at the classical site or a cathedral, ask the guide what time and where the return pickup point will be, melt discreetly to the back of the crowd, let the rest of the group obediently follow the guide and then go off in the opposite direction to explore on your own. That way you can absorb the magical atmosphere without being attacked with every known fact about Olympia or El Greco by a guide who believes that the only way to get a good mark in the final passenger survey is to talk incessantly.

And beware of Christmas cruises. Lovely idea as it sounds, your fellow passengers may be a little off-putting. A crew member explained that many of them fall into the SAGA category – Send A Granny Away. Families who have had every Christmas wrecked by a grumpy granny complaining that the turkey is dry and the roast potatoes are cold reach the point where they can stand it no longer, have a whip round and pay for Granny to go away next December on a Christmas cruise, where she can vent her grumpiness on the crew. On the other hand, if you are a granny yourself, you're getting a bit bored with the family and you fancy a trip to the Caribbean at Christmas, you know what to do.

Cuddles

When Childline was brand new, a teenager found our office. She described the abuse she was suffering at home, and held out her arms to me. I hugged her for minutes on end. One of our staff said to me, 'Many abused children never experience a safe cuddle.' What a tragic loss for any child.

In a happy family there is something so instinctive about a cuddle. Babies depend upon it, skin to skin. Children should be as accustomed to cuddling as they are to breathing. It's the way they greet their friends, their pets, their grandparents, the way they show their joy when their parents return, and they return to their parents. A cuddle is the warmest kind of hug, your arms enclose each other, heart pressed against heart.

As the years go by, life can become too pressured and busy to find room for cuddles. Some older people manage to hang on to their hugging habits. I still remember my grandmother's scent, lavender and talcum, as she enveloped me in lace and tweed. But many literally lose touch even with their nearest and dearest, and instead develop a habit of aloofness. You can tell the spiky, spiny people who guard their personal space and repel all invaders. Sometimes it's because they are far too important to allow such an intimate moment. Sometimes because loneliness has created an almost physical barrier between them and the rest of humanity. Either way there is a sadness about it, so perhaps David Cameron's much-derided suggestion that we should 'hug a hoodie' could be adapted to 'cuddle a granny'. As long as Granny enjoys it, and doesn't find it intrusive.

Dancing

How I envy the lucky people for whom dance is a natural spontaneous expression of joy. For me, dancing has always been like negotiating an obstacle course, as I try and discipline my various limbs to pay attention to each other. People have been known to roar with laughter when I run to catch a train, because all my bits move in opposite directions. It doesn't help that my feet are so big and my legs are so skinny that I look as if I have built-in skis. Poor Anton du Beke had his work cut out in series two of *Strictly Come Dancing*, and rapidly discovered that I have no muscle memory either. He once groaned in mid-rehearsal, 'Esther, you must remember this step, we've done it forty times,' and I had to confess that I didn't. I wish I could dance, but I can't.

But that doesn't mean I don't love watching other people dancing beautifully. I know I've been a bit harsh on ballet (see *Ballet*), because of the long-term damage the training does to professional dancers' bodies. And it's not just coincidence that so many ballroom dancers have their hips and knees replaced. But their sacrifice is our pleasure, because the experience of watching great dancers is unforgettable.

I once sat in the *Strictly* studio and watched Vincent Simone and Flavia Cacace dance the Argentine tango. That is a crazy dance. The *gancho*, or hook, where Flavia kicked violently between Vincent's legs, was so extremely risky that if your partner did to you it would make anyone in their right mind dial 999. And there were moments when they grabbed the back of each other's heads and flung their legs in the air in a way that would surely have them banned from any civilised dance floor. But they partnered each other with such focus and drama and intensity that of course at the end we leaped to our feet, applauding from sheer exhilaration and respect. You can see why if you watch them both on YouTube. And that is a pale shadow of the experience of actually being there with them in the studio. Because dance is like that.

Len Goodman will be long remembered. He was the spine of the show, the one ballroom expert on the first judging panel. And he managed an irresistible combination as Head Judge of being firm, fair and funny.

The achievement of *Strictly* is that some of that heat, energy and connection gets through the camera lenses, so that we at home share the excitement. Some of it. We non-dancers are incredibly jealous of you who can express yourself like that. An amazing talent. And the mystery is that dancers are bought by the yard by professional shows, as if anyone can do it. Well, I am your witness and your evidence: they can't.

Dating

Dating is never easy, however old you are. I remember being 17, when your date would take you home and you would steel yourself against the inevitable smelly, invasive kiss on the lips and his tongue round your tonsils. Then and now, 16 or 60, there is nothing worse than being kissed and fumbled by someone you don't fancy. I used to reach for my keys long before we arrived at my family home, and long for my mother to lean out of her bedroom window and screech, 'Esther, what time do you think this is?' The sad news is that as you grow older it doesn't get any easier.

In my sixties I was commissioned by a magazine to go speed dating on an evening devoted to older women. By 'older' the young men meant 35, not 65. So I was a brutal shock. One of the young men I spent three minutes with was quite sweet, so I asked him why he liked older women: was it the lure of the mature wallet? He said no, he was just hoping for a grateful old slapper.

The trouble with older men, I have found, is that they are very used to being the boss and in control. Brought up in a patriarchy, a patriarchy is where they are comfortable. Partnership is altogether too woke for them. One gentleman I invited to an event and then gave a lift home to had so little faith in my driving that he seized my steering wheel and tried to steer my car for me. I never saw him again.

In my seventies I went on a date with another gentleman of mature years. When he dropped me back to my home, I turned my cheek to him for a goodnight kiss and he seized me by the chin, turned my face to his and plonked one on my lips. I could not say goodnight fast enough.

Then I took part in an episode of *Celebrity First Dates*. At first I had turned them down, but they persuaded me that having launched The Silver Line helpline for older people, many of whom had lost partners, it would give permission for our callers to admit that they would love to find somebody else to share their lives with. So they paired me with a very nice man, an Irish lawyer slightly younger than me, and we had an enjoyable evening. Then they interviewed us both to discover how we thought the date had gone. I said a few nice things about him. When they asked him for his verdict, he said, 'I think, Esther, for a lady of your advancing years you are splendid company.' There was no way forward from that.

I was interviewed by Irish radio the day after it broadcast, who said couldn't I forgive him? It might, after all, have been a joke. I said, 'Never, ever, make a joke about a woman's weight, shoe size or age.' And I stand by that.

Decluttering

It's got to be done. So here's what I've learned. There are two types of human being: the hoarder and the chucker. If you're a chucker you don't need my advice. You have probably already chucked away all the stuff you don't need, you know where your treasures are stored, regularly divest yourself of rubbish as you go along and love minimalism. Well, lucky old you.

If, on the other hand, you are a hoarder like me, you never find anything when you need it, your heart breaks when you throw away a crisp packet just in case it comes in handy in the future and there is hardly room to move in any of your drawers or cupboards.

A professional declutterer told me that hoarders are born, not made. You can tell from the time they are toddlers whether they cling on to their belongings. I know my hoarding is hereditary – in my grandmother's home, if you opened a cupboard you had to stand well back as the contents leaned over you threateningly.

If even you have reached the point where you realise some stuff has got to go, don't try to declutter alone. Persuade a friend to help you, because you need to be draconian or you'll end up struggling to give away one rusty teaspoon.

When I moved from my family home into a flat, my children hired a professional declutterer for me because they realised I was avoiding the issue of what to do with 40 years' worth of stuff. She was a kindly American who threw open a cupboard, counted the contents and said, 'Esther, nobody needs 250 vases.' I replied that nobody ever has enough vases. I hung on to six, but oddly over the months they began to breed again, so now I'm back at 20. All of them vital.

I've downsized twice, so I know the rules for hoarders who have to steel themselves to throw things out:

That much-fabled 'spark of joy' criterion invented by the Japanese expert author Marie Kondo to measure what an object really means to you is not, alas, infallible. A spark can grab you by the vitals every time you pick up a rag or a scrap of paper, which is why you need another pair of eyes, a friend or a professional, to distinguish between a genuine treasure and a bit of pointless stuff.

Decide what you would like to do with any stuff you manage to get rid of. The classic way is to divide it all into three groups, to sell, or give, or throw away. Then label three big bags 'sell', 'charity' and 'dump' and systematically work out what goes into which bag.

Personally, I've never managed to sell anything – the whole internet buying and selling industry baffles me – but I'm sure expert advice exists on the web that can help, if that's what you'd like to do.

Giving things away is much easier, whether it's to local charity shops or into recycling bins. The British Heart Foundation will even take furniture and electrical goods. I know because when I decluttered the first time, to publicise their shops the BHF asked if they could take a photograph of me surrounded by the stuff they were taking off me. I agreed and was surprised to see myself in my local paper that week under the headline £1,000 ICE BUCKET DONATED BY ESTHER. I had no idea that the very heavy, rather ugly yellow ice bucket (which had been given me by a friend but which had never been used) was in fact gold. For a fleeting moment I wondered whether to pop along to the BHF charity shop and reclaim it, but decided against it. It's a wonderful charity, they deserved it, and there was a chance my stinginess might have created a follow-up news story.

Don't get too excited if you decide to sell and assume your belongings have any intrinsic value. An auctioneer walked around my home with a sneer, and in the end broke the bad news to me, that nothing was worth his while to auction because all I owned was 'brown furniture'. I asked him what had so devalued brown furniture and he said, 'Four letters: I. K. E. A.'

Move on. I was once invited to a reception in Buckingham Palace for people aged over 60 who were still making a difference. I was delighted to see my friend Sir Nicholas Winton there (see *Winton*), who had saved a generation of Czech Jewish children from the Holocaust. To my surprise I saw Queen Elizabeth walking towards us, and I introduced Sir Nicholas to Her Majesty. I told her his story, how when the war prevented his wonderful humanitarian work he put the children's documents in a briefcase in his loft and forgot about it. It was only when he was decluttering and his wife discovered the case that he told her, and they set about finding the children and returning their pictures and papers to them. (That's when we told his story on *That's Life!*, which has now been viewed millions of times on Facebook and YouTube.) I ended the story by saying, 'So, Your Majesty, he forgot about it for years.' 'Quite right,' said the queen. 'Much better to move on.' So I pass on that advice to you. Things are things. Having decluttered, don't waste time missing the stuff you don't own any more. Do what the queen did all her remarkable life, and move on.

Decor

Fashion is a peculiar syndrome. When I was young, Art Deco was the most unpopular style. Now it's highly desirable again, so I remember the matching dressing-table and wardrobe my parents got rid of, walnut wood with typical 1930s angles and curves, and wonder why I ever thought they were ugly and didn't buy them myself.

My own taste has changed so much over the years. I remember the sixties for brown hessian on the walls, and I furnished my first home with fake Tiffany table lamps you couldn't give away now. Currently I live in a cottage with decor I love, flowered chintzes at every window and on each chair. A million miles from the fashionable minimalist greiges and blacks and whites as you could imagine. One of my family absentmindedly estimated that they would have to spend at least a hundred thousand pounds to modernise it. Over my dead body.

So enjoy what you like, whatever fashion dictates. The only problem will arise when you decide to sell your home and you have to 'stage' it for someone else. Then completely ignore your own taste; that can't be the arbiter. Someone I know lived in a nice, cosy home in a fashionable part of London where oligarchs and Middle Eastern oil billionaires choose to live. However, their house was not attracting the offers my friends had in mind. So they took their estate agents' advice and changed everything to suit the buyers' taste instead of their own. At huge expense they made the doorways higher, gave every bedroom its own walk-in wardrobe and bathroom, put a pool, a flat and a wine cellar in the basement, and lo! They sold it and made the most ginormous profit.

But if profit is not your object, my friend, the comedian Cyril Fletcher gave me a different but valuable piece of advice. If you have a special day, he said, spending time somewhere lovely which makes you particularly happy, buy something. It doesn't have to be expensive. Just something you can put on a sill or a table so that you glance at it from time to time, because it will constantly remind you of past happiness. And that's not really about decor, is it? It's about keeping around you memories of the best moments in your life.

Death

My dear friend, the comedian Cyril Fletcher, who joined me on *That's Life!*, advised me never to make a joke about death because once past a certain age death is not funny. Now I am as old as he was, I agree. But I have recently been reminded of the work of a Jekyll and Hyde poet, Harry Graham, who wrote sentimental lyrics like those of 'You Are My Heart's Delight', but also many bloodthirsty poems which I remember from my childhood and which still make me laugh, such as these two:

'Aunt Eliza'
In the drinking-well
(Which the plumber built her)
Aunt Eliza fell, —
We must buy a filter.

'Tender Heartedness'
Billy, in one of his nice new sashes,
Fell in the fire and was burnt to ashes;
Now, although the room grows chilly,
I haven't the heart to poke poor Billy.

My grandmother particularly liked that one. You can find them in Harry Graham's collected works, *Ruthless Rhymes for Heartless Homes and More Ruthless Rhymes*. But be careful who you read them to. Maybe safer to stick to 'You Are My Heart's Delight'.

Delivery

Once upon a time – you may find this hard to believe – there were retail palaces in the centres of our cities called Department Stores. And you could wander through their beautifully lit areas, where the goods were artfully placed to tempt you and skilled assistants were waiting to help you track down exactly what, until then, you had no idea you wanted. Or maybe that was only in John Lewis. But that was the world BCS. Before Covid Struck. Now, things you think you may need arrive by van to your door. And in my case turn out to be nothing like my hopes and dreams. Right now I have twenty new bras, all hideous, and all far too tight. So what has prevented me finding the nearest retail palace and swapping them for the right size? I have been seduced by delivery to my door. It's such a luxury. Not to worry about parking. Not to try to find the right person and ask the right question that will lead me to the right article. Just click and hope for the best. Will we ever enjoy shopping again?

Dementia

So many illnesses and disabilities fill us with dread, but this, according to surveys, makes us the most frightened. Every now and then there is a glimmer of hope that the cause and eventual cure will be just around the corner. Let's hope so.

Dentistry

The only thing worse than going to the dentist is surely being a dentist. Can you imagine having to pick around someone else's teeth, inhale their bad breath, hook out pieces of old food?

When I had to undergo a good deal of dental surgery, my dentist told me he would give me Valium to withstand the many hours it took. I refused, on the grounds that I was breastfeeding. He was nonplussed at first but consulted a colleague in the States, and then said he'd ply me with alcohol instead. I remember arriving in his consulting room: he threw open a cocktail cabinet and gave me the choice. As it was seven in the morning, all I could cope with was vodka and orange. So he gave me a large slug of it. I can only tell you that it put me off vodka and orange for life. So I suppose undergoing dentistry might be a way of combating alcoholism, but I don't recommend it.

Desmond

My late husband, who died far too young aged 69. He was funny, generous, sensitive, kind and we miss him desperately. But of course it is better to have loved and lost than never to have experienced this love, so I feel immensely lucky.

Diana, Princess of Wales

We owe so much to the risk-takers, the rule-breakers. Were it not for them, we would never have discovered that fire can be tamed to cook food, or that water can be swum and sailed across. We'd never have a single Impressionist painting. But they pay a heavy price. Diana, the Princess of Wales, broke the rules governing what princesses may and may not do. Her book and her *Panorama* interview were egregious examples, but not the only ones. And in the end she risked her life, and lost it.

It was a major loss, not only for her family, especially her sons, but also for the world. Without her campaigning, there would have been no world ban on landmines. And who knows how many other important causes she might have spearheaded, had she lived, instead of dying, aged 36? The same age that the other icon, Marilyn Monroe, also died. Were they two victims of the way we use and abuse beautiful women? Or were they victims of their own risk-taking?

When Princess Diana died, because she had been so supportive of Childline, Childline volunteer counsellors were asked to walk in the procession behind her coffin, and as president of Childline I was given a ticket for the funeral service in Westminster Abbey. Before it started, I spoke to some of the crowd, including a homeless woman who had slept all night on the pavement outside Westminster Abbey to make sure she had a place at the front, having come from Glasgow to be there, because, she said, 'She cared about us.' And she did. Diana cared about people who thought nobody cared about them. People with AIDS. People living in cardboard boxes under a bridge. So I'm not with the cynics who dismissed the reaction of the crowds lining the streets in London, weeping, leaving flowers, lighting candles, as 'hysteria'. It was grief. It was loss. It was real.

I first met her very soon after she married Charles, at an event in London for GLAD, the Greater London Association for Disabled People. She said to me, 'Why are you here?' which seems to be one of the regular questions royalty use, along with 'Have you come far?' I replied that having well-known people involved with a charity or an event sometimes helps to publicise their work. She said, 'Yes, that's what my husband says.'

Childline launched on 30 October 1986 and within a few weeks we received a cheque for £200 from Princess Diana – a personal donation. (The other celebrities who gave us personal donations were the prime minister, Margaret Thatcher, who quietly pulled out a personal cheque from her famous handbag when she visited us, and the singer George Michael, who gave us all the royalties from his fabulous hit 'Jesus to a Child'.) When we moved to Islington (Childline had started in a tiny office in the shadow of St Paul's Cathedral, which we rapidly outgrew) we invited the princess to open the office.

She walked round meeting our staff and volunteers, and I saw her silhouetted against a window. She was as slender as a reed. I remember saying to her lady-in-waiting, 'Gosh, she's thin,' and the lady-in-waiting saying hurriedly, 'Yes, but terribly fit.' Which of course she was not.

Emma, one of the children who had been helped by Childline, gave Diana a bouquet, and as she took the flowers she said to Emma, 'Are you glad you contacted Childline?' To our distress Emma said, 'No, it was my job to suffer.' Her father had been sent to prison for abusing her, and she blamed herself for the catastrophe to her family; the newspaper reports had shamed and humiliated them to all their friends and neighbours, and they were suddenly on the breadline. I met Emma when she was adult, and by then she realised that it hadn't ever been her job to suffer, that her father was responsible for the crime. But in that one sentence she had demonstrated to us and to the princess how abused children all too often blame themselves.

Incidentally, they say a picture is worth a thousand words. When Diana's visit ended there was a huge crowd of postmen waiting to see her leave, and she whispered to me, 'I'd better say hello, otherwise I'll get into awful trouble.' She went over to them and started to shake hands with the front row, they all threw their hats in the air with joy and that became the picture on the front page of the *Mirror*, with a story about the posties, but nothing at all about Childline. So inviting a huge celebrity in the hope of attracting the media and spreading awareness of your charity doesn't always work.

On another of Diana's visits to Childline, I introduced two boys we had supported to the princess. It was years before the era of selfies, and I was alarmed to see that they had brought a camera with them, which I thought wasn't allowed. But when she came in and saw it lying on the table, she said, 'Does someone want a picture?' Of course they said yes, and they still treasure that picture. She was like that.

When she launched our Tenth Birthday Appeal for Childline at the Savoy Hotel, she made a speech about children being our future, and I introduced her to newspaper editors and other influential people who only attended our event because they wanted to meet her. Incidentally, one thing I have learned about royal visits: everyone gets furious. Are they going to be introduced to the royal? Will they get proper precedence? It's a nightmare. But it was worth it for the friends we made and the funds we raised as a result.

She was the most celebrated woman in the world, but Diana also did countless secret acts of kindness. As I discovered when I was making *Hearts of Gold*, a TV show which handed out gold heart-shaped brooches to unsung heroes for their acts of kindness or courage. One day Rebecca Handel rang and said she wanted her children to be given our awards, although she stipulated that we had to keep it secret and couldn't show it on the programme. She explained that when she had been pregnant with her second baby, Bonnie, the baby had not been thriving in the womb. So (this was in Canada) before she was born Bonnie was given an intra-uterine blood transfusion. It was before HIV/AIDS had been identified, so the blood was not tested. Tragically, it was infected, and the virus was transmitted to

My A–Z of surviving almost anything

baby Bonnie. The virus was also passed on to Rebecca and her husband, but not to Bonnie's elder brother, Joshua.

Although Bonnie had health issues, it took years for HIV to be diagnosed. At that time, everyone was so frightened of catching the infection they refused to play with HIV-positive children or meet their families, so Rebecca insisted her illness must stay secret. She said I had to drive to their home by myself to present the hearts of gold to her children for their bravery.

I made the journey alone late one winter evening, met the family, and then went up to see Bonnie, who was extremely ill, lying in bed, with oxygen to support her breathing. On a shelf was a framed and signed picture of Princess Diana, and Bonnie showed me a four-page letter from her. Rebecca had written to the princess explaining what had happened to the family, and Diana had sent a handwritten reply to Bonnie.

Bonnie was finding it difficult to sleep, so I sat on her bed and made up a story for her. 'This isn't really a bed,' I said. 'It's a boat, and I am rowing us across a lake. It's very dark; the only sound is the gentle splash of the oars, and I am rowing towards an island in the middle of the lake. There's a full moon, and the moonlight is painting a silver pathway for us in the darkness. As we get close to the island, we see that it is covered with white rose bushes, and coming down between the roses to meet you, who do you think it is? It's Princess Diana.' Bonnie always remembered that story, and so did I. Very sadly, a couple of years later Bonnie died. Then, when Diana herself died, her brother Charles decided that she would be buried at Althorp, their family home, on an island in the middle of a lake there, where he planted bushes of white roses.

However, I don't believe in predicting the future, and I certainly don't believe I'm psychic. But that is what happened.

After Bonnie died, Diana kept a connection with the family. When Rebecca's health worsened and she grew very ill, I went to an event attended by Princess Diana and warned her that I thought Rebecca was dying. A few nights later, the princess went to the hospital to find her, but very sadly she was too late. Rebecca had just passed away. So the princess gave the flowers she had brought to one of the other mothers in the ward. She sent a bouquet to Rebecca's funeral with a message saying, 'To a wonderful mother.'

But like her son Harry, in spite of the difference their fame had enabled them to make, eventually Diana found the price was too high. I attended the lunch held by the charity Headway where the princess made her last speech, announcing that she was going to give up most of her public life because the press intrusion into her private life had become impossible to bear. A documentary, *Diana: In Her Own Words*, includes parts of that speech, but it doesn't show the moment when we all gave her a standing ovation. The charities represented there wanted to show her their gratitude for everything she had done for them.

A few days after that speech I was telephoned by Centrepoint, who were opening a new children's refuge in Islington. They said that Diana had been booked to make their speech at the opening of the refuge, but although she would still attend, she could not make the speech in public, so would I instead? I accepted, but that was one of the most intimidating invitations I've ever received.

On the day it was pouring with rain, and when the princess arrived there was no lady-in-waiting or anybody else to help her; so she seemed a lonely figure, drenched, and looking around for somewhere to put her wet umbrella. She was introduced to the mayor, who was an elderly lady, and the mayoress, who was her four-year-old granddaughter. They sat together in the front row. I started to speak, but I could see the little girl was fidgeting and bored. So Diana opened her handbag and let her look through all the contents, taking out her lipstick and her compact, which kept the little girl happy. I can't imagine any other royal doing that.

Later I met the heart surgeon, Professor Yacoub, who told me that she used to visit his wards unannounced very late at night, to cheer up the children who had operations and couldn't sleep. She used to bring bottles of nail varnish and paint their nails different colours. He said you could see them visibly change, eyes brighten, smiling, their immune systems picking up. It is said she thought she had healing hands, and he thought so.

When Princess Diana died in 1997, we were rung at dawn by a friend to tell us. We switched on the television news and couldn't believe it. Like the rest of the world, we were stunned. Gradually the details came out, that she was going by car through a Paris tunnel being chased by photographers on motorbikes, and she wasn't wearing a seatbelt. Her bodyguard had survived the crash, but she and Dodi Fayed had both tragically died, along with the driver of the car, Henri Paul.

At her funeral I sat in a section of Westminster Abbey with rows of people who worked for charities she supported. I was a few rows behind her private secretary, Patrick Jephson, and when her coffin arrived I saw his shoulders crumple as he broke down. Charles Spencer, her brother, gave the eulogy, which praised her, of course, but was filled with anger. He felt that the media had hunted her to her death, and the royal family had not protected her. When he finished, through the open door of the abbey we could hear a sound like waves breaking. The crowds outside watching on big screens were applauding his speech, because they felt as he did, and it was a relief to hear him express their anger for them. As the sound of the applause rippled up the aisles of the abbey, we in the charity section were the first people to join in. The sound of our applause rolled up the abbey to where the royal family were sitting, and with everyone else applauding, some of them began to clap as well. But not all.

After the service I walked with other charity workers to Kensington Palace, where there were mountains of flowers. On the way I met some photographers carrying their cameras and ladders, and for the first time they looked really guilty. When I reached the palace I remember reading some of the labels and looking at the flowers, which were wrapped in shiny cellophane so they glittered in the sunlight. Then I went home.

What did I learn from Diana? That given how crucial pictures are to the media, beauty exerts great power. She was so tall, with intensely blue eyes and extraordinary glamour: she outshone everyone else in the room, on the screen or on the page. Her suffering made her sensitive to

My A–Z of surviving almost anything

others. She reached out to vulnerable and dispossessed people, physically touched them, listened to their stories and remembered them. She was intuitive and empathetic, and that combined with her beauty meant her campaigns, such as the banning of landmines, were uniquely effective. That history is written by the survivors. So no matter how much she wanted to have her say on *Panorama*, because of the revelation of the underhand methods of Martin Bashir it has now been suppressed.

And that some rules should be obeyed. You should always wear a seatbelt.

Diet

At my most sensitive age, from teens to early twenties, I was fat, and hated it. So I was constantly but unsuccessfully on diet after diet. I went on the low-carb diet, the high-protein diet, a diet I invented myself of cauliflower, cottage cheese and grapefruit, which put me off those for life, but nothing worked. Then I joined Weight Watchers and they taught me about calories, and slowly the excess pounds dropped off and stayed off. That coincided with an adrenaline-fuelled career, so I can't be sure which worked more effectively.

We investigated slimming claims on *That's Life!* and discovered that what you really need for any diet to work is an incentive. For the programme we invented the olive diet, where you eat what you like, but always precede it with an olive, and at the end of the week get yourself weighed on a television programme. It worked like a dream, but whether it was the olive, or the knowledge they would be weighed in front of an audience of millions, we couldn't decide. My advice from my investigations, my own calorie counting and the experience of my friends, is beware of alcohol. That glass of wine can accidentally double your calories and undermine your willpower. Sorry.

A few years ago I went to look around Oxford with my daughter Miriam. I showed her my old college, Somerville, and as we were leaving I saw to my amazement my old dean, Miss Hervey, walking towards us. She was responsible for disciplining us students and can only have been about ten years older than us at the time, but had a great talent of seeming middle-aged, so we thought she was at least 50 when she was in fact only in her thirties. As she came past my daughter and me I exclaimed, 'Miss Hervey!' and she stopped, stared at me and said in her snootiest don's voice, 'Who. Are. You?' Immediately I was 19 again. 'I'm Esther Rantzen,' I said meekly. She stared even harder. 'You can't be – Esther Rantzen was *fat*.' And she strode on. My daughter had been paralysed with shock, but came round to ask me 'Who was that rude old lady?' 'That wasn't a rude old lady,' I explained. 'That was an Oxford don.'

It cheered me up to know that Oxford dons hadn't changed, but I had.

Dogs

Bad enough when arbitrary standards of beauty dictate to women what they should look like (see *Beauty*), but what about dogs? They haven't any choice. Ears and tails are cruelly cropped to fit our ideas of beauty. In our desire to create 'beautiful' pedigrees we inbreed them so they inherit disabilities like hip dysplasia. Because we think it makes them look cute, we insist that pugs' noses are so squashed that they can hardly breathe through them, that bulldogs' heads are so enormous they can't give birth normally, that bloodhounds have such deep folds in their faces that they get infections in the grooves, all because we breed them to follow what we decide is beauty.

Don't assume that things are improving with more so-called 'designer dogs' or 'planned hybrids' being bred and sold, like cockapoos and labradoodles. In fact, people who breed them are hoping to create new pedigrees from these mixtures. There's too much money in the dog trade. The Kennel Club, who are the arbiters of pedigrees, have taken steps to try to stamp out the callous, greedy puppy farmers, who make huge profits from the inflated value of pedigree puppies, treat the breeding dogs appallingly badly and sell unhealthy puppies, but it's a big problem to solve.

For years the Kennel Club presided over a pedigree system that led to an explosion in the value of dogs with inbred disabilities. How much better it would be now if they did away with pedigrees entirely, and we simply judged dogs on their physical and mental health. But obviously that won't happen. At least they do now promote mongrels by hosting Scruffts, the Crufts for cross-bred mixtures. After all, the late Queen Elizabeth who was patron of the Kennel Club, loved her 'dorgis' (dachshunds mixed with corgis). And nobody could be more passionate supporters of the idea of pedigrees than her family.

Dress Codes

They are, thank heavens, loosening. Traditionally, if a man turned up to a formal occasion wearing something different from everyone else, it was a catastrophe. Whereas if two women turned up at an event wearing identical dresses, that was a disaster.

Some years ago Desmond and I were attending a glitzy charity ball where Princess Anne was the guest of honour. I was wearing a new evening dress by Frank Usher - cream chiffon, strapless, with a matching stole - and we arrived first. Second to arrive was Bruce Forsyth and his gorgeous wife, Wilnelia, who is an ex-beauty queen; very tall, very beautiful, and wearing the identical dress. We looked at each other in horror, because we were due to be standing beside each other in the receiving line for the princess, and as I was at least 6 inches shorter than Wilnelia and infinitely less glamorous, I knew I'd be mocked.

Luckily Bruce took charge (his catchphrase, 'I'm in charge', was accurate and well-deserved). He swiftly rearranged us so that he and Desi stood between Wilnelia and me, and she (being used to this kind of event) took her stole and wrapped it like a scarf around her neck to make the two dresses look as different as possible. And it worked. Nobody else noticed. When the princess arrived I told her what had happened, and at least that gave us something to talk about. Those who know say that royals enjoy minor glitches like that.

But times have changed a bit. Fairly recently I was asked to speak at an event at my college, honouring the principal. I realised that she and I were wearing the same dress, so I kept my coat on until I got up to speak. Then I slowly removed the jacket to reveal the dress, and claimed it was deliberate, to pay tribute to her as a role model.

These days people are less judgemental than they were when Michael Foot was sternly rebuked for wearing a donkey jacket on Remembrance Sunday. It might have been politically inspired, but then the etiquette at funerals and memorial services is strictly monitored. When the queen died, everyone on television had to wear black. Even dark colours, like a burgundy tie, provoke rage among viewers. I was once ticked off for wearing a red scarf at a memorial service.

Rightly or wrongly, we do judge people on their appearance. My husband Desmond told me that when he worked for the *Daily Mirror*, the journalists were told they must always look respectable: men had to wear suits, because they had to prove the tabloids should be taken seriously. And they never knew when they might be sent out to cover a death or meet some VIP.

Before sustainability became trendy, I once wore a 15-year-old dress to a British Academy Awards ceremony and was voted the NAFFTA at the BAFTAs. So I may not be the best person to hand out advice about clothing. Especially as since Covid my favourite garment is a onesie.

Education

Avidly watching quiz programmes, as I do, I am struck by the contrast between the extraordinary specialist knowledge demonstrated on *University Challenge* and the absence of ordinary culture shown by contestants on nearly all the other quiz shows. What is the world coming to?

And here's another question I cannot answer. Around four hundred years ago, William Shakespeare wrote the finest plays ever created. Since then we have discovered a universe of new information, and each generation of children has learned extraordinary new facts to inspire and enlighten them, but nobody has since written a play to rival *King Lear* or *Twelfth Night* (sorry, Shaw, Sheridan and Stoppard). So has our education, short on the classics, short on philosophy, stifled our children's creativity by concentrating on filling their memories, rather than stimulating their capacity to ask questions and debate? Could anyone now write a line to rival 'To be, or not to be?'

Entertaining Children

These days from a worryingly young age they only need a mobile phone or a tablet to be entertained. But beware. A police officer once said to me, 'If a strange man walked in through your front door, up the stairs, into your daughter's bedroom and shut the door, would you allow him to be alone with her? And yet that is what you do each time you allow a child to go onto the internet without you knowing what, how, and with whom.'

So instead I recommend a few old-fashioned party games:

The Sweet Game (although if your dentist is worried I suppose you could play it with something a bit healthier, like fruit). It takes a bag of sweets, and a group of children, I suggest five or more, aged 6–10.

One child goes out of the room. The host empties a generous handful of sweets on the (clean or covered by a tablecloth) floor. They all kneel around it.

One of the children picks a sweet to be 'It'.

The child outside is called back in, is given a bag to put their sweets in and then points at each sweet in turn. As they do, the rest of the children say, 'Yesssss' and the child takes that sweet and puts it into their bag, until the child picks the one the rest have selected and then they all shout, 'NO!' and the child leaps with shock and is allowed to take that one but no more.

Then another child goes outside, and another child picks another sweet to be It, and so on until everyone has had a turn, and maybe the unluckiest is given a second turn. The advantage of the game being that nobody goes away without at least one sweet in their bag.

Drawing Consequences – a version of Consequences for those not comfortable with reading and writing, ideally played by a group of 4–8 children, aged 5–12 years old, each with a pen or pencil and piece of paper. Everyone draws the head of anything, and folds the paper forward to hide the head itself but leaves the neck sticking out. They pass it to a neighbour who, without unfolding the paper, draws the body and arms of anything, connects it onto the neck, folds the paper forward only leaving the top of the legs sticking out, and passes it on. Their neighbour draws the rest of the legs and feet, folding the paper over to hide everything and passing it on, and their neighbour then writes a name on it, folds and passes to the next person who undoes it all and admires the whole picture. Our fridge is covered with the resulting portraits, to our infinite family amusement.

Consequences – the same in theory, only with words. Each person in the group fills in the blank, and folds over the paper and passes it on. The traditional story is:

MASCULINE NAME ....
met
FEMININE NAME ....
while they were ....
He said to her ....
She said to him ....
The consequence was ....
And the world said ....

Strangely, I have no memories of my family Consequences descending into pornography.

The Post-it Game is one where you write the name of a well-known person, stick it to a guest's forehead, and they have to discover who they are by asking questions, to which the answer can only be yes or no. This is a great icebreaker.

Charades. The trick is, if you have a really talented mime at the party, not to guess the subject too quickly.

Then there are a host of games produced by the marketing companies attached to the various games on television, some of which are great fun, and have added glamour through their TV connection.

The great advantage all these games have over 'screen time' is laughter.

Europe

Two of my closest friends voted the opposite way from me in the 2016 Brexit referendum. We've learned not to discuss it. The independence referendum in Scotland also provoked fury on opposing sides. Next time a politician suggests a referendum, whatever the issue, I suggest we turn it down, for the sake of our friendships.

Evil

Burke may not have said, 'For the triumph of evil it is only necessary for good men to do nothing', but it's true. Although I would say good men and women.

Exercise

Lordy, I'm so tired of experts pointing out how important exercise is. I know some people enjoy it, and they doubt-less do a lot of it. For me, unless it's a walk somewhere gorgeous, it's intolerably boring. Funnily enough, if you look at Dr Google there's plenty of stuff about the nasty conditions caused by too much exercise. And I remember a survey of older people which concluded that exercise in later life is very good for you – provided that you don't fall over. So the only kind of exercise I do is to stand up straight, or as straight as I can manage, and breathe deeply.

If you fancy moving around a bit, my advice is, wear trainers. Forget the rude things that used to be said about little old ladies in tennis shoes. Dame Joanna Lumley (see *Lumley*) wears trainers, and she can do no wrong. Follow her examples and wear glamorous trainers in gold and silver, studded with jewels. They are miles easier to walk in than anything with a heel, and they don't come off.

Never go downstairs without holding on to a banister (see *Falls*). Have a bath rather than a shower (sorry, Greta, it may be bad for the planet, but see *Falls*). Don't run unless you're escaping something nasty, like an avalanche, and even then it may outrun you, so is it worth it? And seriously limit the amount of alcohol you drink (also see *Falls*). I know I'm biased because I've never been an enthusiastic drinker, and I realise that people get real pleasure out of that glass of red at the end of a long day, but have you noticed how enormous today's glasses are, compared with the small but perfectly formed glasses our parents used to drink from? Why not buy yourself some little retro cut-glass goblets, dirt cheap because they are not dishwasher proof, and drink out of them instead.

Experience

My first job in television was as a researcher for producer Ned Sherrin, the creator of television satire programmes in the sixties, and discoverer of David Frost and Roy Hudd (and me). The programme he created was exciting, and mischievous, and I loved every moment. When that series ended, my second job was working for the brilliant but barmy Derrick Amoore, the editor of the nightly programme *24 Hours*. He frankly hated working with women and told me so. He said, 'Your problem is, Esther, that I like working with people with bits that stick out and I don't understand people with holes.' And his regular greeting to us with holes was 'Take your knickers off.' I didn't.

But he did give me a job, filing 23,000 black-and-white photographs, which took me three months and from which I was released by his deputy, Tony Whitby of blessed memory, who may have said to me – during my imprisonment with three enormous filing cabinets and a PA called Philomena Peckett, a beauty queen from Zanzibar – to cheer me up, 'No experience is wasted.'

If it was Tony who said that to me, thank you. That has been engraved on my heart ever since.

No experience is ever wasted. Even those tedious, frustrating three months filing photographs were worthwhile, because they taught me the value of a challenging job, and never to take it for granted if you are lucky enough to find one. Looking back over the past sixty or so years, there have been many other moments you would think I would or should regret.

Like taking part in *Strictly Come Dancing* when I have absolutely no muscle memory and was voted out in week three. No, because without that I would never have met my fabulous friend Anton du Beke; witty, talented, always entertaining and a loyal supporter of Childline.

Or like taking part in *I'm a Celebrity...*, living in mud and using the nastiest loo I've ever encountered outside China. No, I loved every moment of it, having my phone and watch removed, getting up with the sun and going to bed with the brightest stars I've ever seen. (In the sky rather than the stars who took part. I was in a group which included the very successful presenter Robert Kilroy Silk, who kept losing his temper. This made the viewers vote for him to undergo a good few ordeals, which made him even crosser.)

Do I regret the experience of spending £15,000 standing as an independent candidate for Luton South in the general election of 2010 and losing my deposit? No, I made real friends who helped me and my charities hugely, and I'll never forget the privilege of attending the count, and hearing the slap, slap of little bits of paper as every single vote was counted by hand.

E

Even lockdown had its moments, as for the first time I could watch the seasons change in my garden and learned how to use Zoom.

So no experience is wasted. Although I haven't tried death yet.

Experts

Another Rantzen Rule: 9 out of 10 people doing any job are hopeless at it. The trick is to find the 1 in 10 who is a genuine expert and is really good. This matters more with brain surgeons than plumbers, but matters with both.

Fairy Tales

When Diana Spencer married Prince Charles on 29 July 1981, the Archbishop of Canterbury told them, and every-one watching around the world on television, 'Here is the stuff of which fairy tales are made ... but fairy tales usually end at this point with the simple phrase "They lived happily ever after."' So in reality, do all fairy tale marriages, Diana and Charles, Cinderella and her Prince Charming, end in tears? Did Diana wish she had never become the world's most famous and admired woman and danced with Travolta? Did Cinders wish that she had never gone to the ball and stayed home sweeping the hearth instead?

So to ensure that our children understand the differ-ence between fact and fiction, and to prevent their minds being tainted with false hope, should we all stop telling our children fairy tales, and certainly give up believing they can come true? Or should we follow Albert Einstein's advice: 'If you want your children to be intelligent, read them fairy tales. If you want them to be more intelligent, read them more fairy tales.'

I'd rather side with Einstein. Because when as children we hear how Cinderella's kindness was rewarded by her fairy godmother, and how the prince woke Sleeping Beauty and rescued her (worried about consent? Oh, please ...) these tales implant in us nice and early the ideal of justice, and teach that the good are rewarded and the bad are punished and what goes around comes around. And even if real life turns out to be tougher and harder, these fairy stories allow our children to dream an unlikely dream, and one or two may come true. And that allows them for a moment or two longer to believe in magic.

Maybe as we get older it is inevitable that we become more cynical. But if we stay alert, we still can recognise the magic around us in the real world; it's just that it takes on a different disguise. When the first buds start to appear on the bare branches, isn't that magic? When a new baby grasps your finger, isn't that magic too? It may not involve an abracadabra password to open the treasure cave, or the wave of a wand to turn a rat into the footman, but it revives hope in our hearts. And hope is the sunlight that makes life worthwhile.

And I find it reassuring that even in these tough times people are still writing, reading and loving fairy tales. Thank you, J.K. Rowling, Disney and Julia Donaldson for making sure today's children still have magic in their lives. And also thank you, local theatres around the country, for preserving the fairy tales of Cinderella, Jack and the Beanstalk and Mother Goose at pantomime season.

My own childhood was enriched by the Victorian and Edwardian fairy stories I read, from *The Water Babies* to *The Cuckoo Clock*, and *Harding's Luck*. The authors, Charles Kingsley, Mrs Molesworth and E. Nesbit, took me on a trip deep into my imagination, and while I read and reread them, the Victorian and Edwardian worlds they created entirely surrounded and absorbed me. Their stories warned me about issues of cruelty and poverty that, luckily, I didn't have to face in my secure, suburban, childhood in the1940s and 1950s.

So I'm certainly with Einstein.

F

Falls

According to official NHS figures, around one in three adults over 65 and half the people over 80 will have at least one fall a year. Don't do it.

Fathers

A good father is invaluable in showing his children that strength can be used gently. I get worried when some commentators imply fathers are disposable or irrelevant to the welfare of a child. They matter.

Fear

Obviously we need fear, otherwise we'd drown or burn ourselves to death. However, as I found when injudiciously taking part in *Strictly Come Dancing*, fear can imprison you when you need to be bold and confident. The most frightened I have ever been was playing Dick Whittington in Bognor one Christmas, giving a lecture to Action for Children, and seeing my elder daughter passing out in a fever faint. I froze. So I did when I watched my toddler son gambolling towards the unfenced edge of a castle roof: it took my husband to rush towards him and scoop him up. So I don't find fear at all helpful.

However, when I took part in ITV's *I'm a Celebrity... Get Me Out of Here!* I learned a way to pretend to be calm and courageous which I have since found useful in combating fear. When Mike Tindall, the royal rugby player, took part in *I'm a Celebrity...* he said, 'Fear is a choice.' Well, it can be.

You can refuse to allow your mind to notice the reality around you and divert it somewhere else. During the programme I was locked in a coffin underground and then showered with creepy-crawlies, and currently I believe I hold the record for staying down there without shouting to be released. Forty-seven minutes. I did it by persuading myself I was in a warm cosy bed on a cold November night, and that the bugs were children and I was telling them the story of Cinderella. I strung it out as long as I could, and managed to ignore the fact that by the end the insects were creeping all over me. Martina Navratilova only lasted 30 seconds. Then I was voted out for failing to peel potatoes. She stayed in for weeks. Which proves that quality wins out in the end.

Feet

Treasure them while you can still reach them.

Fingernails

I find a vitamin D supplement makes all the difference to their strength and resilience.

Fish

Now that I own a small pond, I've discovered how intelligent goldfish are. The next time you hear someone claim that they have incredibly short memories, defend them. You only have to watch them playing tag with each other, or hide-and-seek, and you can see their individual personalities. And they have excellent memories.

Fishnet Tights

Strangely sexy. On women.

Flowers

Wedding bouquets, funeral wreaths: flowers are the most eloquent way to say thank you, and congratulations, and I love you. They mark very special moments in our lives – perhaps the way they fascinate and enchant us is not just due to their beauty, but the fact that they are so ephemeral. Gather ye rosebuds while ye may, Old Time is still a-flying. Artificial flowers last for ever, but no matter how skilfully they are made they are charmless by comparison. And the more delicate the bloom, the lovelier they are.

My grandmother Emily forgave me every sin, except picking wild flowers and throwing them away. She taught me to treasure flowers of every kind, and filled her garden with magnificent delphiniums I have never been able to grow in my own. In tribute to her I have managed to fill mine with native wild flowers: bluebells, primroses, cowslips and even a self-seeded orchid.

Do not think, however, that wild flowers are easy to incorporate into your garden because they are native to our soil and our climate. They are also extremely picky. I had many failures before I noticed that my lawn was in fact a wildflower meadow if I allowed it to grow and blossom, instead of mowing it. And I still don't know whether the poppies and cornflowers I would love to surround my olive trees will consent to bloom there.

For me, the flowers in my garden are especially precious because they are inextricably connected to the passing of time. The thrill of the first snowdrops spangling the grass makes my heart lift. There is a gorgeous local churchyard where the tussocks of rough grass are iced with these delicate white blossoms, their heads drooping elegantly, a wonderful signal that spring is tiptoeing in under the chilly February clouds. But I hope I'm not xenophobic; I equally welcome immigrants from the East, early camellias and rhododendrons bringing into my garden an exotic dash of pink and white with them from the Himalayas, contrasting against the pale blue of a spring sky.

Then a procession of golden trumpets, daffodils and narcissi, spring to attention under my hedges and along my drive. The brilliance of tulips arrives like an explosion of scarlet, black and purple, some frilly, some stylishly plain, filling the flowerpots and beds with colour. I love combining them with forget-me-nots and lobelia so they can flare against a blue background. And at last, roses. Hanging in clusters from an arch, covering a bush with scented mop-heads. My friend the gardener and comedian Cyril Fletcher used to say that fragrance is the soul of a rose.

F

To pick or not to pick? My cousin Edie used to gather huge armfuls of rhododendrons and arrange them in her house, explaining to me that the height of the flowers above the vase should always be twice the height of the vase itself. My rhododendrons come and go too fast for me to bring them indoors. And I get very frustrated when I pick the hydrangeas late in the summer and put them in water, only to find in less than an hour their petals crumple. So I offer this advice on preserving their blooms a little longer.

Make sure the water in the vase is room temperature, not too cold. Add a drop of liquid soap, and a teaspoon of sugar. Cut the stems on a diagonal, and plunge them quickly in boiling water before you put them in the vase. And that should keep them going for a few more days. But you can enjoy them for weeks longer if you leave them to bloom on the bough.

My A-Z of surviving almost everything

Food

My children say I only enjoy the food that was around in the 1950s. And it is true that I cannot stand innovations like wraps: to me that's like eating face flannels. Nor do I enjoy sushi. Why eat damp, cold, raw fish? However, I have grown to tolerate pizzas and avocados, both popularised in the sixties, so I'm not a complete food Luddite. I am delighted that Paddington, particularly in his interview with the late queen, has popularised marmalade again. Though I prefer it spread chunkily on hot buttered toast rather than in a sandwich stored in a hat or handbag.

While I'm being nostalgic, it's decades since I was offered delicious hot rice pudding with a thick brown skin the way my mother used to make it. And whatever happened to the junket I was given when I was very young? Does it still exist? I seem to remember that it was slimy but tasted nice sprinkled with nutmeg. And where are the other war-time treats, like the pink, sweet rosehip syrup that stood in for orange juice when oranges weren't available? And malt extract, thick black stuff that oozed out of a jar and stuck to the spoon? So my children are quite wrong to say I'm stuck in the fifties. More like the forties.

Friends

I used to be amazed at the difference between male and female friendships. All men seemed to need was that a friend would buy a round when it was their turn. Women need so much more. A similar sense of humour. An absence of judgement, or lack of competitiveness. To be honest about whether your bum looks big in this, but not too honest. To be imaginative and if possible generous at birthdays and Christmases. To be there on the phone or over a cup of coffee when crisis strikes. So much more.

And if the worst happens, you will be surprised who actually stands by you when you need someone. Almost certainly it won't be the people you assume are your true friends-in-need. Desmond and I once helped a friend out financially when he was in bad trouble. It killed our friendship stone dead, not from our side. When I moved and downsized from a house to a flat I discovered that every man I knew made for the hills and hid, and all my female friends strapped on their aprons and sprang into action helping me pack and unpack boxes. However, if I need a lift or someone to escort me to a red-carpet event, it's the men in my life that are prepared to drive me there or help with an umbrella. So maybe that's about different gender skills. Or just status.

Friends is also the best-loved American comedy series. The writing, the performances, the production are all, to my eye, flawless. The great thing is that it is constantly running on one channel or another, so when all else fails, which it often does, we can switch back to our favourite group of characters and be enchanted yet again, even if we do know the script so well that we recite it with them. Could such a set-up ever happen in real life, without the wonderful humour injected by their team of writers?

The consoling thing about watching Rachel, Monica, Phoebe, Joey, Ross and Chandler is that they never change. The downside of growing older in real life is that you may outlive some of your favourite people; over the years I have lost a couple I miss desperately. Grief, said the queen, is the

F

price we pay for love. It's also the price we pay for friendship.

Fringe (Edinburgh)

When people talk about the law of unintended consequences, they usually mean unexpected disasters. They
rarely point out that there are just as many wonderful
unintended surprises. Take the Edinburgh Fringe Festival.
Nobody planned it; it just started spontaneously with eight
groups arriving uninvited to the first Edinburgh Festival
in 1947, and from that acorn the magnificent oak tree of
talent has grown. I was exceptionally lucky to appear at
the Fringe in a late-night Oxford student revue in 1960.
We were camping in dormitories in the Freemason's
Lodge on Johnston Terrace near the castle. Our revue was
in a church hall, the Cranston Street Hall, and I remember
one night after our performance climbing to the top of
Arthur's Seat, the hill towering over the city, and watching the sun rise, and then scrambling down and being
given bacon and eggs by the very kindly local grocer to
cook for breakfast. No wonder everyone loves Edinburgh.

1960 was the year *Beyond the Fringe* opened in the
Lyceum Theatre, rocketing Peter Cook, Alan Bennett,
Dudley Moore and Jonathan Miller to instant stardom.
Alan was working as an academic at the time, and knew
members of the Oxford Theatre Group, the company I was
in. He came to visit us one day, taking refuge from his own
rehearsals, and talking gloomily to Romola Christopher-
son in the hall. 'It'll never work,' he said, and explained
that there were disagreements in the cast. (A brilliantly
funny performer, Romola decided to have a serious career
in the civil service, including working for Mrs Thatcher in

Number 10 and in the Department of Health, where it is said that her party turns were legendary.) So we decided we'd better all go to their first night in the Lyceum, so they had someone in the audience to applaud them and laugh. As it turned out, we weren't required. The theatre was packed, and every joke, sketch and monologue took the roof off. Their irreverent mockery of sacred institutions, religion, politics, public school education, was familiar to us students but sent a gale of fresh air blasting through traditional revue targets: wives, mothers-in-law, gay men. Amazing looking back how misogynist, homophobic and racist the accepted humour had been until then. Their show transferred to the West End and then from London to Broadway, and changed comedy for ever.

The Edinburgh Fringe continues to discover new talent and creates a glorious anarchy, especially in comedy. Walking down the Royal Mile in August is a joy, as cheerful over-optimistic students thrust leaflets into your hand, begging you to watch them that night. Other festival Fringes exist, of course, but Edinburgh is unique.

Fringe (Forehead)

A clever device many of us use to hide wrinkles and save money on Botox. The fringe that has reached a remarkable height of fame and controversy is Claudia Winkleman's.

The F Word

My beloved Aunt Nancy used to work in a day nursery in the East End of London in the 1950s. One day a member of staff came over to her holding a small boy by the ear, and said, 'Miss Leverson, Georgie said the F word.' Nancy looked sternly at him and said, 'Georgie, I don't know what the F word is, but you must never say it again.' From then on, Aunt Nancy told me, she was regarded by the staff as a saint.

But none of my family knew, or used, the F word or any other four-letter words. My mother and her sisters had been strictly nannied, educated in girls' boarding schools, and growing up and mixing with respectable middle-class families, nobody used such vocabulary. I never heard them until I went to university.

But with the sixties came liberation and suddenly the F word was everywhere. Listen to nearly all today's comedians' punchlines and you will find they depend on the F word to provoke a guffaw. The miracle of Billy Connolly is that, rude as he is, and he is, little old ladies come out of his show wreathed in smiles and totally unshocked, because alongside his F words is amazing creativity. But he is unique. Too often the four-letter words are there to make up for the fact that otherwise the joke is not funny.

I was present in the control room the first time the F word was used on television. Ken Tynan, the theatre critic, said it in a debate about censorship, and Huw Wheldon (the managing director of BBC Television) defended it as being 'germane' to the debate. When Ken said it, the producer Ned Sherrin swung round in his chair and said to us minions sitting behind him, 'Is that some kind of record?' It was, and as I was the researcher he made me collect all the cartoons in the papers next day and pin them on his board. That's how great an event the F word was then. Not any more.

Fun

When we launched The Silver Line helpline for older people who needed somebody to talk to, I discovered the killer question 'What do you do for fun?' And way too often the answer was 'Fun is just for young people', or 'I haven't had fun for years'. Well, they should. If I were prime minister I would bring in a law stating that everyone must have fun at least once a day. I remember when we were piloting The Silver Line in Jersey, and we were taken to visit an older lady who was disabled. She lived in a nice apartment, she had a view of a communal garden and once a week she was taken shopping by taxi, but that killer question stumped her. She watched other people having fun, she never had fun herself.

But there is a simple solution, because a friendly phone call once a week, sharing a joke or a memory, can become the fun both parties can look forward to. Especially if they don't have many enjoyable conversations in their lives, and things can get a bit serious and worrying for all of us if all you can think of is problems mounting up with health, wealth or loneliness.

Funerals

Very tough. And they get tougher as one gets older, because there are more and more of them among our friends and families. I always promise myself that I won't go to any more. But I do, of course (see *Memorial Services*). I have decided I would like to be cremated, for space and conservation reasons. I know that the worst moment during the funeral service is at the end when the coffin, which has been sitting there grimly throughout the service, glides away and disappears through the curtains. At which point I have asked my nearest and dearest to arrange that the chapel sound system either breaks into The Doors' hit 'Light My Fire', or Vera Lynn singing 'Wish Me Luck (As You Wave Me Goodbye)'. Anything to cheer up the congregation.

Besides jokes, the other way to distract a mourning congregation from their grief is by making them angry. The funeral for my cousin, a distinguished psychiatrist who had been born Jewish but became Buddhist, was taken by the chaplain of the hospital where he worked. The chaplain was very high church C of E, which pleased neither the Jews nor the Buddhists in the congregation. Especially as he referred to my cousin throughout as a physiotherapist.

I remember my husband Desmond recounting to me what happened at Hughie Green's funeral. It seems that discord had broken out as the funeral cortege set out, with people arguing about which flowers went on the coffin etc. As people arrived at Golders Green Crematorium, they were surprised to see huge TV dishes in the car park. Then one of the speakers, Noel Botham, revealed in mid-speech that Hughie had a secret celebrity daughter, a love child who had become one of the biggest stars on television. So whatever else that funeral was, dull it was not.

Fur

Personally, I don't wear it. You may ask what's the difference between me happily wearing leather shoes, bags and jackets, and objecting to wearing fur, and you have a point.

Gardening

There is every chance that by the age of 60 or 70 you will have had enough of people, which is when plants take over. No wonder King Charles talks to them. They don't judge, don't patronise, and they will reward you with blossoms and fruit if you throw manure at them. But beware: plants are as picky as people, and the best-laid plans will be frustrated by a flower that refuses to flourish where you want to put it.

I always wonder whether TV gardeners, like many TV cooks, cheat and rely on willing serfs who do the hard work, while all the star celebrity does is let them do the digging and comes in afterwards to sprinkle a trowelful of topsoil and take the credit. Like the home economists behind the scenes in cookery programmes who supply the perfect plates, measure out the ingredients and do all the washing up.

Garden Centres

In the days when people used to pay by cheques, the owner of a garden centre told me that because his customers were gardeners they were too honest to bounce theirs. Wouldn't it be nice to believe that?

Gnome Nobbling

More than fifty years ago, somewhere around 1968, I was working on a show called *Braden's Week*, for the first time appearing on screen as a researcher/reporter. My colleague, the wonderful John Pitman, was the film reporter, while I was relegated to street interviews, which I then did for more than forty years, and always enjoyed hugely (in spite of having been nicked by the police for it – see *Arrest*). However, John was busy elsewhere on location when our producer found a story in the newspaper about gnome nobbling. So I was instructed to investigate, as my first job as a film reporter.

According to the paper, a phantom gnome nobbler in the gardens of Folkestone had been terrorising the gnome-loving population by nobbling their gnomes. So my producer told me to ring the stringers who had written the story, the local Folkestone journalists, and arrange to meet them there. I did. They didn't sound at all keen, but I mentioned a fee, and that cheered them up enough to agree to a meeting.

When I arrived with the film crew in Folkestone the two stringers introduced me to my first interviewee, a St John Ambulance officer, whose connection to the story appeared flimsy. It just seemed to be that he was a friend of the two young journalists and he had rosy cheeks, a rosy nose and sticking-out ears, so he looked rather like a garden gnome. I had a predilection for puns so I asked him if he thought it was a politically inspired attack, an 'Anti-Vietgnome demonstration'. He said seriously that he thought not. After the interview I asked if he had noticed my pun – he said yes, but he just assumed it was my mispronunciation.

Then I met our main interviewee, a lady who refused to be interviewed face to camera. So we only showed the back of her head. She explained to me that as she had a plethora of gnomes scattered around her garden in full view of the road, she had added a strand of barbed wire to her netting fence, and she insisted on not being identified in case the nobbler recognised her and followed her home from the supermarket. She owned a Hammond organ, so we filmed her playing 'Gnome Sweet Gnome'.

Then our film director, James Clarke, bought a gnome and dropped it into the sea, filming it as the waves lapped around it. He dubbed on poignant music. James went on to become a very successful porn film director, but that was much later.

As James and I drove home discussing the story we realised that we had neither seen a nobbled gnome nor heard of one. So it occurred to us that perhaps the stringers had been driving around Folkestone complaining that nothing ever happened there, had passed our interviewee's garden with its huge crop of gnomes and together invented the story of the phantom nobbler. Which the lady made come true, or at least true enough for our film, with her fear of being followed home by the phantom. And that would explain why the young journalists hadn't been at all keen on us coming down to Folkestone with a film crew to investigate.

But that taught me about the difference between written journalism and film-making. It's far easier to invent a story in print than it is on film (but see *April Fools*).

When the programme transmitted, Bernie Braden and I had a conversation in the studio after the film, and I asked him if he was a gnomosexual. I wonder if that would be regarded these days as gnomophobic?

Grammar

This is blood pressure time. Mine soars with rage each time I hear people wrongly and with mistaken grammatical snobbery using 'I' when they should say 'me'. As in 'Come to drinks with Peter and I', 'Send an invitation to Dad and I' or 'Why don't you join my wife and I?' Grrr. It's 'Me', darling, you wouldn't say 'have a drink with I'. So you shouldn't say 'have a drink with Peter and I'.

Then there's mispronunciation. Not mispro*noun*ciation. Not tor*toy*se. Not mis*chiev*ious. Wrong, wrong, wrong.

Then of course there's the constant problem of the over- and under-used apostrophe. 'It's' means 'It is', as we know. Never the possessive 'my cat refuses to sleep in it's basket'. Or the greengrocer's favourite: POTATOE'S £1.20 A BAG.

And the highly irritating and unnecessary preposition. Why do people these days have to 'meet with you' or 'meet up with him' or 'park up here'?

And why, oh why sprinkle 'like' throughout our conversation, and start every sentence with 'So ...'?

The reason is that language is constantly in flux. Otherwise we would all speak like Chaucer's Canterbury pilgrims. Maybe one day it will be perfectly grammatical to use I instead of Me. Maybe the apostrophe will become extinct. Perhaps more and more prepositions will encrust our language, and So will replace Well, and we oldies will just have either to control our infuriated peaks of blood pressure, or keel over and die of rage and grammatical fury. Is the apostrophe worth losing your life over? For me, like, yes.

Grandchildren

It is said that you love your children, but you are in love with your grandchildren. I was so sure that would never happen to me. I watched tough old bats who were friends of mine turning into puddles of sentimentality, pulling out pictures of their grandchildren, picking them up from school and boasting about their GCSEs and I vowed that I would never dissolve into that puddle of love. But I did.

There is an infatuation that overwhelms you when you have grandchildren; they put a spring in my step, they constantly make me laugh, I cannot say no to them, and when invited I find myself squashing myself into home-made forts, or galloping around a garden seeking treasure at considerable risk to life and limb.

In this I am replicating my own relationship with my grandmother. She taught me patience (the card game, not, alas, the virtue), and Victorian rhymes and music hall songs. When as a stroppy teenager I ran away from home it was to stay the night with her and have meringues for tea; when she needed drops in her eyes I stayed to minister to her. It was pure, unconditional love. But everything has its price, and something called grandparent alienation is becoming more and more common. Alongside the fact that grandparents are often crucial when it comes to school pickup time or helping out with holidays or mortgages, there is the threat that if the marriage or part-nership breaks, or there's just a rough exchange of views, the grandparents may be cut off.

These days separation and divorce are so common that when they occur, and tragically sometimes even when bereavement happens, many children not only lose one parent, they also lose those grandparents. But grandpar-ents have sometimes been the only continuity, the only unconditional love, the only place of safety. So it can be a major loss for the grandchildren.

For the grandparents, too. When they are cut off without even being able to send a birthday present or a Christmas card, grandparents tell me it feels like a living bereavement, and grandchildren have written to me to say how desperately sad they feel sometimes not even being able to say a final goodbye. There have been campaigns to try and strengthen the law to protect children's access to their grandparents. So far without success. Even when there have been Members of Parliament who understood how crucial this relationship can be for the whole family, when the moment comes to consider legislation, once again older people's issues get kicked into the longest, most distant grass.

So I believe we need a minister with specific responsibility for older people's welfare. They could support the rights of older people across the board: social care, transport, health and access to grandchildren, among many other issues. Including the digital switchover, which is excluding so many older people. Until we get a minister, the voices of older people will go unheard and people in their forties will carry on blithely making decisions for people in their eighties and nineties which exclude or diminish their rights. In the 1960s it was the other way around and there was a Yoof revolution. Maybe now we need a Toofless revolution. Just a thought.

Grey

If you are in your mid-thirties, tall, thin, tanned and blonde, you can wear as much grey and black as you like. But as the years go by and your colouring fades, maybe you should adopt pastels, salmon pinks and sky blues, lemon yellow and apple green. Just to prove you're not the ghost of your spritely younger self.

My A–Z of surviving almost everything

Grief

I have already quoted the late Queen Elizabeth's message to a memorial service in New York after 9/11, saying that grief is the price we pay for love. Apart from that, I have very little useful advice. I'm not sure any advice is useful when you lose someone you deeply care about.

I remember that quite soon after my husband died I hosted a talk show for young widows, and they told me the one rule they would like me to emphasise is that there are no rules about bereavement. They described the experience they all had endured, that they had found their friends and families were incredibly judgemental, telling them they should get out more, or less, should cry more, or less, move house or stay where they were, start dating again or don't. The fact is that we all have to find our own way to grieve. While I'm quoting royalty, the queen mother was supposed to have said when she lost her husband that you never get over it, but you do learn to behave better. Perhaps.

Grumpiness

The popular stereotype of the grumpy old man or woman: how true is it? Do we really grow grumpier as we get older? We certainly get firmer in our views, know what we like and what we abominate. And it may well be that as life ahead gets shorter, we resent wasting time with excess courtesy. But the very worst age for grumpiness is surely male adolescence; you're lucky to get more than a grunt or a click from boys between the ages of 15 and 20.

For the rest of us there are several antidotes to grump-iness. Sunshine. Chocolate. An unexpected bunch of flowers. A surprise party. Billy Connolly or Mel Brooks. Silk pillowcases.

Money, sadly, doesn't work. Some of the grumpiest people I know are the richest. What does Elon Musk do as a treat? Send a tweet?

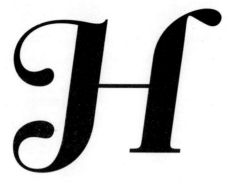

Hahaha

Oh, the joy of the uncontrolled, uncontrollable laugh, when the eyes stream and you clutch your stomach and bellow (see *Heroes*). You do have to be a bit careful to time your guffaws sensitively, but honestly, when something hits your chuckle button, as Ken Dodd used to call it, there's nothing you can do to stifle it. I remember once I was walking to school with a friend when a pigeon dropped a message on her, and as pigeons don't do anything by halves I laughed for about twenty minutes. Our friendship was never quite the same. No wonder so many television clip shows depend upon that kind of accident: *schaden-freude*, as Germans call it, pleasure in someone else's pain.

It's better still when a joke is deliberate rather than an accident. When some great comedian provokes that kind of laughter they hold a special place in our hearts, don't they? We really love them for it. Take your pick of the geniuses: be they Tommy Cooper, Les Dawson, Eric

Morecambe, Billy Connolly or Victoria Wood, we remember the hilarity they created and it feels as if they extended our lives.

And they do. The Mayo Clinic in America has listed the many ways laughter is physically good for us. Laughter can increase oxygen intake, they say, which can stimulate the heart, lungs and muscles. Laughing releases endorphins, the feel-good chemicals our bodies produce to make us feel happy, and it can relieve pain or stress. Laughter can even boost our immune system response through the release of stress- and illness-reducing neuropeptides.

No wonder when a comedian tries to make us laugh but fails we want to kill him. No wonder the comedians themselves call that terrible moment when an audience turns against them 'dying'. The mystery is, since laughter is so life-enhancing, why is it that these heroes who can fill our grey and gloomy day with a moment of sunshine don't get the honours they deserve, the knighthoods and the damehoods? Why weren't Dame Victoria, and Sir Eric, awarded the highest honours for all their services to fun?

Hair

Hair arouses strong emotions. I understand why Samson was passionate about his long hair, since his strength depended upon it until Delilah treacherously trimmed his while he slept. Which is why he lost his superhuman strength, was captured and blinded by the Philistines, and was only able to wreak vengeance on them when his hair grew again and he pulled the pillars of the temple down and killed them and himself. Understandably, he was enraged by that haircut. But why do parents get so angry when their sons grow their hair or their daughters shave theirs off? Why do Jewish ringlets and Rastafarian dreads have such great symbolic significance? Why did Elton get so insistent on hair transplants when he wore so many hats anyway?

Hair is closely associated with ageing. Not just the baldness that many men try to stave off with transplants, dyes and potions, but the way it turns grey and grows long and bristly in eyebrows, and arrives in unexpected places such as nostrils and ears and falls out from other places where one has been accustomed to see and or shave it. So perhaps that's another reason we watch its progress with dread.

The truth is, I find I can only feel confident if I'm having a good hair day. It must be something in our DNA. Like the way a male peacock feels about his tail. So I suggest that if you have a big occasion coming up, you make sure you get your hair done by a hairdresser you trust first.

Happiness

Is happiness chemical? There can be mornings when you wake up feeling bright and cheerful even if you are on your own, are in the middle of a power cut and have run out of milk. On the other hand, sadness can also be completely irrational and unrelated to events; it just hits you in the pit of the stomach with no trigger. Perhaps being prone to sadness is due to something that happened to you in the womb (a mother's place is in the wrong, see *Mothers*) or maybe being swaddled (which I think explains why Russians grow up to believe they need a tsar, a Stalin or a Putin to keep them strapped together).

But what is the secret of happiness? A rabbi was once quoted to me as saying, 'How's the toothache?' And when you reply, 'I haven't got a toothache,' he answers, 'Well, aren't you grateful that you haven't got a toothache?' So gratitude may be an integral part of happiness.

The other definition of happiness came from a godson. I asked him when the happiest time in his life was, and he said it's that ten minutes after the alarm wakes you and before the time you have to get up, when you can snuggle down and enjoy every stolen minute. Ever since he said that I have really appreciated those moments, and maybe that is the secret of happiness. Trying to appreciate every moment. Especially if you haven't got a toothache.

My A–Z of surviving almost everything

Harry

When Prince Harry was a working member of the royal family, I saw him in action several times, and met him once. He had his mother's star quality, her warmth and empathy, and a special gift for talking to vulnerable children. He achieved so much in a short time. As well as all the good causes he supported, there is the charity, Sentebale, he co-founded for children in Lesotho, and he found a visionary way to use his army experience by inventing the Invictus Games to give hope and encouragement to disabled veterans and showcase their courage and resilience. Like everyone, I was delighted when he found a wife. Meghan showed that she too has a personal touch and can raise awareness and much needed funds for charity, helping the Grenfell Tower victims to create a best-selling cookbook, for example, and working with Smart Works, the charity which enables women to find work and dress appropriately for job interviews.

In 2018, when Harry handed out the prizes at the London Marathon, I spoke to him about his concerns about children's mental health. He absolutely understood the issues young people were talking to Childline about. Why didn't I recognise that he was talking from personal experience? Overawed by speaking to a royal prince up close and personal, I never properly analysed what he was telling me. Nothing prepared me for the revelations in his book, *Spare*.

Although I have listened to hundreds of very distressed children who have contacted Childline over the years, I never suspected the agony William and Harry had experienced was still there, raw and unhealed. And yet the adult Harry has described the horror he feels when he hears the click of a camera, sees their flashes go off, and is reminded yet again of the moment his mother lay dying, surrounded by paparazzi.

When Princess Diana died in 1997, her sons were so young I assumed that Harry and William would have had all the support they needed to help them deal with the tragedy and trauma of losing her. The royals must have called in the best possible professional experts, surely. Or taken advice from excellent charities working with bereaved children, like Winston's Wish.

But it seems not. Instead of therapeutic help, the boys suffered the destructive impact of the demands made by us, the public. I'm sure we all remember how both princes were told to meet the crowds, to admire their gifts of flowers and messages, then notoriously to walk behind Diana's coffin, a moment that I found deeply moving at the time and only now recognise as intolerable cruelty. As they grew older, both were targeted by the press and the paparazzi (whom I describe hunting their mother, see *Paparazzi*).

Worse was to come once Harry had married. The media have a well-established pattern of first building you up, then knocking you down. And there were some who found this useful. Harry says there were those among the Palace staff who protected senior royals by leaking negative stories about himself and Meghan to use instead, Meghan has described it as 'feeding the wolves'. I know this can happen in corporate communication departments, as it did in another organisation a friend worked for – the difference being that she could contradict any published falsehoods, while Harry says he was silenced.

And the blizzard of attacks had a brutal effect upon Meghan, especially when they both had to attend a charity performance by Cirque du Soleil. I was in the audience that evening. Once again, I admired their smiles as they arrived, and assumed they enjoyed the spectacular show. I had absolutely no idea that once in the safe darkness at the back of the Royal Box, Meghan had collapsed in tears, feeling suicidal.

Some commentators have chosen to disbelieve her description of her deep unhappiness. But then some have also denied the claim that there has been any racism in the media attacks on Meghan. Very soon after the photo-call to introduce their first baby, Archie, to the world, I had a conversation with a photographer who works for the national press. He told me how furious he and his colleagues were with Harry and Meghan. I asked him why, and he said it was because they couldn't see the baby's face. I said, 'But you could see him in Meghan's arms, and his little head in its hat.' He said, 'What we wanted to see was what colour the baby was.' Curiosity? Or conscious or unconscious bias?

When *Spare* was published, the press almost unanimously attacked Harry for writing it, and claimed he was 'whingeing'. There were very few positive references to the revelations it contains. Until I bought and read it myself, I had no idea Harry has donated £1.5 million of the money earned by the book to his charity, Sentebale, and another £300,000 to the British charity for gravely ill children of which he was a patron for 15 years, WellChild.

I hope wounds within the royal family will heal, and Harry and Meghan and their children can find the peace and happiness they need to thrive. It will need us all to appreciate them as sensitive humans who have been badly hurt by our insatiable desire to pursue and publicise them. If we just blame them without learning from them, that will be an opportunity lost, because of course the royal family, and the country, could gain so much from 'spares' as talented as them.

Yes, let's focus on the good causes they throw a spotlight upon, yes, let's hold them to account. But not at the expense of their survival. And if Harry needs an apology for our mistakes – Harry, I am truly sorry.

Health

It's the only thing that matters. If you have a chronically ill loved one, as I have, the impact of their illness on them and their lives is horrible. But even if you take all the proper precautions, don't smoke, drink moderately, take exercise, avoid dangerous drugs, look both ways when you are crossing a road, health is still a gamble. The healthiest friend I had, who ate carefully and followed all the other fitness rules, died incredibly, tragically young.

I was always interested, when signing up with a new doctor, that they would consistently ask me the same question: how old were my parents when they died? When I said 90 and 94 they lost interest in me. So that's the best health advice I can give you: pick your parents carefully. Genes rule.

Help

In the beautiful book *The Boy, the Mole, the Fox and the Horse*, the Boy asks the Horse what is the bravest thing it has ever said, and the Horse replies, 'Help.' It can be difficult to ask for help when you need it. According to the Beatles, age makes a difference. Their glorious song says that when they were younger, so much younger than today, they were more self-assured, but as they grew older they realised they were feeling down and needed help. It does take confidence to admit that. Especially if you are suffering any kind of mental health issue. It's far easier to ask for help with a broken leg than a broken mind.

Even when the help you need is momentary, we can be reluctant to ask. The cliché is that men won't ask someone for directions if they have lost their way, and like many clichés it is often true, so that must be deeply rooted in the male machismo. As a woman I have no problem at all asking directions, or seeking help to change a tyre. Or to wallpaper a room. But if I'm involved in writing, or designing a Christmas card or appealing for a charity I care about, I am as stubborn as any lost man refusing to ask for help. Why?

I suppose it's all about our own sense of identity. I've come across people who are reluctant to ask for help keeping their homes clean and tidy, because they know how they want it to be done and don't believe anyone else can do it their way (see *Cleaning*). I have a friend who resisted employing a cleaner for years, and when I asked why, told me that she would never be able to find anyone who would clean the skirting boards with disinfectant the way she did herself. So obviously these are folk with admirably high standards. As I have admitted, I am such an incompetent cleaner that I am grateful for help from anyone with any skill at all to keep grime at bay.

So my advice is, forget your pride and machismo. If you need help, ask for it. Unless of course you have good reasons not to. My experience with Childline and with The Silver Line has uncovered a couple of reasons which have validity. One is that asking for help can make things even worse, as abused children found in the past. And the other is that even well-meant help can bring about a situation that you didn't anticipate and don't want, and it can be difficult to put things back where they were. But those circumstances are, thank heavens, comparatively rare. So I say, if you need it, ask for it.

Heroes

Odd how humans need heroes. Like packs of wolves, we need leaders. And we are dangerously easy to manipulate by someone who wants power and will promise us anything. There are many dangerous fake heroes, who were - who are - real villains. I leave you to suggest current examples.

So who are the genuine, copper-bottomed heroes? In the olden days, they were created on the fields of battle. Boadicea, Henry V, the Duke of Wellington, and in our time, Churchill. Their courage, their leadership, has made them immortal.

There is a peacetime hero we can all unite to respect: Nelson Mandela. His authority was built through suffering and his magnanimity was unrivalled. I remember well the day he was released from prison after 27 years; when an interviewer asked why he was not angry, he said, 'As I walked out the door toward the gate that would lead to my freedom, I knew if I didn't leave my bitterness and hatred behind, I'd still be in prison.'

Part of his wisdom was that he recognised the value of setbacks: he said once, 'I never lose. I either win or learn.' And, most apposite of all in this age of Twitter, he pointed out that 'resentment is like drinking poison and then hoping it will kill your enemies', and 'courageous people do not fear forgiving, for the sake of peace'.

I hope that you have heroes in your own life, people you have watched making a real difference. And maybe you are a hero to others, acting as a role model and inspiring those around you. If so, you may never know how much you have achieved, and are achieving.

And while we are still remembering Mandela, let's also bear in mind that other piece of advice he offered us: 'Tread softly, breathe peacefully, laugh hysterically.'

Hoarding

I don't want to go on about it (see *Cleaning* and *De-cluttering*). As I have mentioned, often, I am aware that I am personally fighting a constantly losing battle against it.

Holidays

Take them. Memories of time spent with the people you love or exploring wonderful new places will last your lifetime.

Home

There are two conflicting meanings for the word 'home'. One is the place you live, where you feel the most comfortable, home being where the heart is. The other being the place to which you are consigned when you are too old, or too frail, or both, to look after yourself.

When I was one of the least successful independent candidates in the 2010 general election, I was contacted by some of the staff of an old people's home in Luton and invited to visit and look around. While I was there, admiring the many activities the residents were enjoying, one of the nurses told me that most of the older people simply could not have survived in their own homes, would not have had the good food, the company, the physical help they were enjoying in the residential home. She told me how dispiriting it was for dedicated staff there to be treated as the last resort, the residential home being described as a terrible fate to be avoided at all costs. And I took her point.

There may come a time in any of our lives when we have to give up living in our own homes and move to a residential home. If that time comes, we just have to learn resilience. And remember that the stuff we had to leave behind was just that, stuff. I'm talking to myself, here, you realise.

Honesty

Said to be the best policy, but is it? I'm not sure any negotiation, or friendship, or love affair, or marriage would survive if we were always honest.

Honours

They arouse such powerful emotions. Which is daft, because rationally we all know that they are arbitrary, that many people who work tirelessly for others are never recognised, and that some people are completely undeserving of the honours showered upon them.

Here's what I have discovered about our honours systems. In order to be recognised, it helps enormously to be connected with an organisation that can nominate you. You may be saintly and deserving, but even if you are achieving miracles as an individual you may never receive an honour. You need the clout of an organisation behind you.

Does a damehood or a knighthood make a difference? Sometimes. If you are connected with a charity, or have some other figurehead role, it does make your visit or your contribution seem a bit more distinguished.

Does it make it easier to get a good table in a sought-after restaurant? It can do. My late husband used to love eating in a particular pub on the River Thames (he told me that whenever the *Daily Mirror* bought exclusive interviews with some celebrity they wanted to keep secret they used to put them up in this pub, and as he worked for the *Mirror* before he came into television he knew whereof he spoke) and the maître d' there always used to call him Sir Desmond. And my husband always used to correct him. In a whisper. When he was walking away.

When people ask me whether having been made a dame made a difference to me, I always say it transformed my life. Because ever since I have regularly been introduced as Dame Edna. Even on the radio.

I knew Dame Edna Everage well and she is one of my role models. Barry Humphries worked on the television programme which gave me my first researcher job, and in which Mrs Edna Everage appeared, dressed dowdily in a woollen coat and hat from the BBC's stock wardrobe, and Barry and I were fond but irregular friends ever since.

When Edna (by now Dame-d and a Superstar) had one of her sell-out West End shows I went backstage afterwards. She was getting changed and her manager came and chatted to us while we waited. I congratulated him on the part of the show where Edna climbed into a swooping hydraulic lift and was hoisted right up to the ceiling of the theatre to harangue the 'paupies' in the upper circle. The manager said that Barry was too scared of heights to rehearse that bit, but Edna hadn't a fear in the world: she leaped into the hoist and swooped around with glee. In fact she had to be persuaded to wear a safety belt.

H
___

People said the same of the genius impressionist Mike Yarwood; that he was a mild and gentle man until he took on the role of Harold Wilson, so he used to drop into Wilson's voice whenever he wanted to rebuke someone or have a row. So the answer to fears and phobias is obviously to take on a different persona. Preferably that of a dame or a prime minister.

If you, or someone you know, deserves an honour but has been denied one, remember the story of the two Harry Corbetts. One was an actor who was a campaigning member of the Labour Party and played Harold Steptoe in *Steptoe and Son*. The other was a magician and the inventor of the much-loved puppet Sooty. When Harold Wilson decided that the Labour supporter Harry should receive an OBE, by mistake the Honours Committee sent notification to the Sooty Harry. So they both received the honour in January 1976. And a good thing too.

One last thought about the gloriously funny, tragically missed Barry. When Adrian Mills and I made a podcast called *That's After Life!*, we interviewed Barry, and he was hilarious as always. Adrian asked him what he wanted to find when he finally reached the afterlife. Barry said, 'A return ticket'. And he revealed that his mother claimed that his first words as a toddler were, 'More please!' We all long for more from Barry, don't we, and just wish that return ticket could bring him back to us.

Horses

However one defines it (see *Beauty*), nobody could be impervious to the beauty of horses. Which is not to say that everyone wishes to climb into a saddle, or bet on them, or breed them. Many do. Many don't.

I once made a documentary in a series called *The Big Time* which followed Joan Barrow, a gifted amateur point-to-point rider, training as the first woman to take part in a professional race as a jump jockey. Her trainer was Dave 'the Duke' Nicholson, and we spent an idyllic summer filming them in the Cotswolds. I will never forget the sight of Joan on the back of a huge grey carthorse galloping towards us through the smoke of golden burning stubble. As it turned out, when the day of her race arrived we were all too busy to put any money on her and she won by twelve lengths.

The Duke was a man of very few words; all he ever said to me when I arrived at dawn to watch his horses leave the yard was, 'Don't get kicked.' I didn't. But I have never relaxed in close proximity to horses, and I pass that advice on to you. In spite of the fact that I now live in the New Forest, which is famous for the wild ponies that wander down the middle of the roads and graze in the glades. We keep each other at a respectful distance. As a city child I was 50 years old before I learned to ride, and enjoyed it until the day I very slowly fell off, landing on my head, which may explain a lot. That was my last ride.

How Are You?

Why, oh why does every conversation have to start these days by asking how you are? When we really, truly, do not want to know. We already had an excellent formal opening to any conversation: 'How do you do?' Which did the same job but doesn't require an elaborate answer. Or an answer of any kind. Now you have to hurdle over the conversational obstacle which threatens to sink you both into a detailed description of hearing exactly how you are, which bit is failing, which other bit is being propped up, what you have replaced with titanium and how many pills and potions you are now ingesting, and none of it offers a laugh or a piece of helpful advice – so why share it? In my age group it's known as an Organ Recital, and frankly, other people's organs are of limited interest to me. As are my own. So when people ask me, as they regularly do, how I am: I tell them the truth. I have no idea.

I

Illness

My GP when I was young told me, 'We live in a hostile environment.' So I'm never surprised when illness strikes, I'm just amazed how much we take good health for granted.

Insomnia

Thank heavens for podcasts, especially the dullest ones (see *Podcasts*). Nobody warns you in your youth about insomnia, which is an aspect of growing older that manages to be both boring and irritating. Having spent the majority of my life sleeping at least eight hours a night, in my later years I have had to adjust to waking at two or three in the morning and lying awake for around an hour before dropping off again. My solution is to find a podcast on my phone and allow it to drone on next to my pillow until my anxious mind is hypnotised into acquiescence, and I fall into deep slumber again. Fortunately, BBC podcasts have a setting which turns them off after the time I select, or at the end of an episode. Equally fortunately there are plenty of dull podcasts. And the one thing to avoid is trying hard to fall asleep, because that is a sure way to keep you awake.

Interests

We can all remember how much easier it was to learn new skills when we were young. But don't let that dissuade you, or me, from learning new hobbies and finding new absorbing interests as we grow older, and I don't mean golf. Nothing against golf, if that's your taste. But there are a myriad other things if you look around. One good place to start, if you are no longer in full-time work or looking after a young family, is u3a. University of the Third Age is a network of older people who want to pass on their life experience and skills and hone new ones, so they run fascinating courses for each other. Though the members are retired, in the sense of being paid to work, they have no minimum age, and their membership are knowledgeable, lively people who are happy to teach and learn.

A friend has joined a choir, and as she is now her partner's full-time carer, that gives her a couple of hours of respite and good company. Another friend has joined a food bank and is constantly delighted by people's generosity. An acquaintance has learned a musical instrument and has joined a local orchestra. I'm not saying all this to make you feel guilty, or give you an inferiority complex: what you choose to do is your own concern. But just to offer ideas about what is possible, and what they all enjoy.

Internet

Infuriating when it doesn't work, miraculous when it does.

Ironing

Here's another underrated domestic skill (see *Cleaning* and *Decluttering*). In the days when I used to try ironing, long given up now, I could never work out how to iron a sleeve, or a sheet or a shoulder. I used to know a laundress who was an ironing magician and I would watch her, entranced. In the olden days they used to fill gaps on television with a potter's wheel. I would much prefer watching a skilled ironer.

I

Italy

I heard a story about two film crews. Some decades ago, when Northern Italy had the most successful economy in Europe and Japan had the best in Asia, an Italian crew went to Japan to film life there, and a Japanese crew went to Milan to film there.

The Italians filmed Japanese people rising at dawn, forcing themselves onto bullet trains, chanting the company anthem every morning, working every hour God sent, and showed their film, wonderingly, back home in Milan.

The Japanese shot the Italians enjoying a few hours at work, long wine-soaked lunches, siestas, happy evenings under the stars. Brought the film back to Tokyo and refused to show it because it would cause riots in Japan.

Ivory

I own some I have inherited but I don't love it, and I won't buy any more. I do love elephants.

My A–Z of surviving almost everything

J

Jealousy

People bang on about the ninth commandment. Personally, I am a strong supporter of the tenth, outlawing coveting what your neighbour has. Jealousy, of all emotions, is the most toxic. It destroys your pleasure in what you have and incites you to hate anyone else who has more.

Jewellery

Sparkly stuff is in my DNA: on both sides of my family there are dealers in diamonds. In fact on my father's side there is a great-uncle who once owned Kimberley Diamond Mine in South Africa. I've been there fairly recently, and all I saw was a large hole in the ground where once the diamonds were. Which is a fair representation of my family's wealth.

My grandmother used to love jewellery and used to pin brooches all over herself, and her brother-in-law once memorably said to her, 'Millie, you look like a Christmas tree.' Unlike Granny, I have found as the years have gone by that I've worn fewer and fewer sparkly bits, and have given any of value away. Apart from pearls. Britt Ekland once pointed out that pearls add lustre to mature skin. As we grow older we surely need all the lustre we can grab.

Jury Service

A fascinating experience; I recommend it.

The case I served on was of alleged grievous bodily harm. I won't go into all the details, partly because they were too complicated, partly because as a member of the jury I'm supposed to keep them to myself. But in some ways it was very simple: everyone knew what the weapon was, a very large knife. In fact it was brought at our request into the Jury Room and laid on the table before us.

Everyone knew who had done it. The only question we the jury had to answer was whether it was a deliberate stab, or an attempt to get the victim off the accused's back. I told you it was complicated.

There was an eyewitness who said it was very obviously a deliberate act (the victim nearly died with a stab wound to a major artery in his groin). But eyewitnesses can be wrong. So we decided to re-enact it, using me as the perpetrator, since I was much the same build as the accused, and one of the other jurors as the victim, since he was a similar shape to him. The foreman of the jury, a social worker, had helpfully brought a pencil case with a ruler in it the same size as the knife. So the other juror climbed on my back, I held the ruler the way everyone agreed the knife had been held, and at once it was obvious that the only way I could stab the victim in his groin was with a deliberate sweep of the ruler. Which is exactly what the eyewitness had described. So we convicted.

The conclusion I reached from that experience was that the jury system is magnificent. Every type of person and personality was represented on it. A couple of men thought everyone should have the right to carry a large knife. Another couple thought carrying a knife was always a crime and merited a conviction anyway. There was a lady who disapproved of the whole prison system, so wouldn't convict. And so on around the table: we contained such a wide range of views that we had to ask the judge for a majority verdict, not unanimous, to which he reluctantly agreed. I never discovered what the sentence was.

The law is odd. We as the jury were excluded from quite a lot of legal discussion, and I knew from listening to other trials as a journalist that the judge would then be hearing quite a bit of evidence that was denied to us, because it was felt to be prejudicial. And that was frustrating. But having such a balance of views and life experience on the jury, though not a guarantee of accuracy in our verdict, was at least a genuine attempt at fairness. So my advice is, if anyone tries to do away with jury trials, don't let them. They are crucial to justice.

Just a Minute

I had a dear friend, the actor Nicholas Parsons, who sadly died far too soon at the age of 96 and used to chair this remarkable radio programme. He was extraordinary. He had overcome a crippling childhood stammer, as my late husband Desmond also did, and like Desmond came out the other side with a beautiful mellifluous voice.

Nicholas was brilliant with words, which is the skill he used to great effect in this word game. He was very kind; speaking as one who timorously tried to play the game, he was unfailingly helpful. He was one of a group of my friends who met each year at a Christmas party, and there was always a fiendish quiz. You knew whichever team Nicholas was on would win.

Just a Minute is a rare thing, a perfect format. Invented by Ian Messiter (it is said, on a bus), it lasted fifty years under Nicholas's chairmanship, and still reigns over Radio 4 with Sue Perkins chairing as broadcasting's most demanding, funny panel game. Though *I'm Sorry I Haven't A Clue* and *The News Quiz* are also fabulous listens.

So why does radio succeed in jolting a laugh out of us, even when we are alone, and the weather is cold, and the boiler has given up, and there's nothing appetising in the fridge? Because radio strikes you straight in the heart without bothering your eyeballs. If gloom hits you, turn on the radio and find one of these shows. It won't make your life better, but it will make you feel better.

J
___

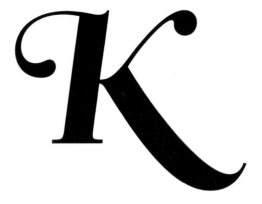

Keys

Get a key board. Not a musical one, the kind you put on the wall with keys on it. Also put a key box outside with a code so that when your nearest and dearest get locked out, they can still get in. So can you.

Kindness

The virtue that really matters. Mends hearts, mends marriages, supports the vulnerable even when they don't seem vulnerable.

Kitten Heels

I have worn them trekking around India. Not any more. Trainers are infinitely safer and more comfortable. No doubt heels are more flattering, especially if like me you have long feet like built-in skis. But with age you realise safety comes first. The most dangerous thing I ever did in heels was to run down the stairs in Piers Morgan's studio. If I'd fallen, would he have caught me? Risky to rely on it.

Knitting

Never learned to, never thought I needed to. However, Michelle Obama, an icon of our time, says that knitting has become one of her favourite activities. So maybe I'm missing something.

Left-handedness

Not to be repressed by right-handed teachers. That can lead to all kinds of problems. And why do it, anyway? Famous lefties, they say, were Shakespeare and Da Vinci. (And me and my grandson.)

Legs

It's strange, looking back to the days when I was young, to see how unselfconscious we all were about objectifying women. I remember when I was 17 going to Paris for French classes in a mixed lycée, and the boys organising a beauty parade for the English girls. We had to walk past them while they judged us on our looks; they were quite well mannered, but definitely objectifying. (As it turned out, Norma, the girl who won, became one of my closest friends at university, and indeed she was, and is, gorgeous. I was green with envy in Paris, but learned to love her when

I got to know her. And when she worked with us as a lead researcher on *That's Life!* she was utterly brilliant, and very, very funny. So the French boys weren't daft.)

In those unenlightened days women were assessed like roast chickens. It used to be said that men either liked legs or breast – and there were ladies who specialised in one or the other. Whereas Betty Grable was renowned for insuring her legs for a million pounds, I recall a lady called Sabrina who appeared on BBC Television's Arthur Askey programmes purely on the basis of her magnificent chest. As far as I remember she never spoke a word. According to an article in June 1955 in the *People*, 'When Britain's now-famous television blonde, Sabrina, made her first appearance earlier this year, she did not speak, sing, dance, do conjuring tricks or even pull faces. She merely slid off the sofa on which she had been lying, clad in a skin-tight black dress, undulated toward the TV cameras and slowly turned sideways-on. About 4 million screens throughout the country were blotted out by a 39in bosom – and Sabrina had arrived.'

I might have liked to be Betty Grable, but I never envied Sabrina. As a teenager I worked out that ladies whose legs were their chief selling point, as against their chests, had nicer lives.

Lesbians

I've never forgotten Miriam Margolyes coming out to me. I'd known and admired her for years, ever since I saw her in a revue when she was an undergraduate. She was so funny. I remember her Twisting as a cave woman. Glorious.

Years later she worked on a TV show where I was the

researcher, and I wrote monologues for her. One day she invited me to tea, and as she sat on a sofa across the room a tremor passed over her face. I was concerned and asked if she felt all right, 'What is it, Miriam, do you feel queer?' That is a word I never used before, and would never use now.

'Yes,' she said, typically honest. 'I am queer.' And then, generously, 'Would you like to hear how I was seduced?'

'No, thank you,' I said as I began to fumble for the keys in my bag, got up, muttered something about another appointment and made to leave. She had a narrow doorway and had to squash past me to open the front door. I have to say she meanly enjoyed my discomfort and squashed past me in every queue and doorway from then on.

For years she was the only lesbian I knew, or knew I knew, and she would tell me stories about pulling her gigantic breasts out of their moorings to amuse taxi drivers. 'I'm trying to cheer up the image of lesbians,' she said, and it was true that in those days they were rather dour.

Not any more. Lesbians are in full bloom, funny and talented as they always have been and no longer hiding their light under a bushel, so to speak. The lesbians I know best and have worked with longest are not just creative and brilliant, but terrific company. All they needed to overcome their dourness, all anyone needs perhaps, is the opportunity to shine.

LGBTQIA2S (so far)

Life is far more complex than it used to be.

Loneliness

I've always needed company. And I've always had it, with my family or at university or flatmates. I've never been alone, until at the age of 71 I downsized from my family home into a two-bedroomed flat in little-old-lady-land. And I didn't like it. No matter how busy a day was, I'd arrive back, stick my key into the lock, and the front door would open into a dark empty flat. Nobody to have a cup of tea with. Nobody to sit next to on the sofa and shout at the television with. So I was shocked to hear myself say to my spiritual daughter (I'm agnostic), 'You know, M, I think God wants you to move in with me.' Fortunately she laughed, and I did what I always do when I need therapy: I rang the *Daily Mail*, and they said, 'Loneliness. Good subject. Write about it.' So I did.

I have never had so much response to anything I've written before. Some people wrote rebuking me for not counting my blessings. 'How can you grumble, Esther, when you've got your health and strength and can travel around? Suppose you were disabled and lived on your own and were imprisoned in the same four walls. How would you feel then?'

Some praised me for my 'courage' in admitting to feeling lonely when there is such a stigma attached to it. I suppose we feel ashamed to confess to loneliness because we suspect that you can only be alone if nobody wants your company. Obviously not true, but we blame ourselves.

Many letters pointed out that there are organisations which are trying to reach out to older people on their own but they are very difficult to target, so how do the WI, the

Townswomen's Guild, the RVS, the churches, the synagogues, the mosques, Age UK, Independent Age, CAMEO (Come And Meet Each Other) and all the other befriending organisations find the people who are suffering from loneliness and give them the friendship and companionship they need?

People told me how destructive loneliness is to their mental and physical health, as I know from personal experience. Why cook when it's only for you? Why go for a walk alone? Why accept that invitation when you have to go there by yourself? Loneliness erodes confidence and increases depression. No wonder the experts say it's worse for our health than smoking 15 cigarettes a day.

All these letters inspired me to write another article for the *Daily Mail*, and I was invited to speak at the conference about the isolation of older people, run by a group of charities under the banner of the Campaign to End Loneliness.

At that conference I remember vividly standing in front of the audience and wrestling with myself not to say what had leaped into my mind. (I always advise people if a light-bulb goes off over their head to ignore it, because if they don't it will take over their lives. It has mine.) I stopped wrestling, gave in, and told the audience that I was experiencing a flashback to a time 25 years before when I had been speaking to a different group of experts. Then I was talking to experts in child abuse, now it was to experts in the care of older people. Then it was about a different stigma, the stigma of abuse, now it was the stigma of loneliness. Twenty-five years before we were concerned about a different group, vulnerable children and young people,

L

and now it was older people. Then, I said, one answer was a helpline, Childline. Could it be that an answer now might also be a helpline? Yes, said my audience, do it.

Well, in 1986 I'd had the skills and connections of a brilliant television team with me. In 2011 I was alone. But I went around the conference taking contact details from everyone who was running a helpline for older people, spent a year visiting them and learning from them, and then reached out to Sophie Andrews as our first CEO, and found the money to employ her, and The Silver Line was born (see *The Silver Line*).

Is there a cure for loneliness? There is no one silver bullet. It takes people working together, and even then, one solution won't work for everyone. But very few of us can survive alone; company is good for most of us. So if you are on your own, make that phone call, dare to accept that invitation, try that meeting, that choir rehearsal, that cookery class. Go for it. If you don't enjoy it, you need never go back. But if you do, it may well banish loneliness, at least for a few hours.

Longevity

Every newspaper regularly offers a recipe for living until you are a hundred. It normally includes eating nuts and beetroot, fasting, cold showers, and inevitably exercise (see *Falls*). What it leaves out is the most important advice of all: pick your parents with care, and choose those who also lived to be a hundred. Nothing like good genes (see *Health*).

However, very few allude to a reassuring survey which showed that the people who live the longest are overweight. Not morbidly obese, because we know that puts a strain on heart, knees, everything. But just pleasantly plump, so that if flu or Covid strike, you have a few reserves to draw on until you recover. So I would add to these longevity recipes: don't deny yourself the choccy biccy that cheers you on a rainy day.

Loss

I believe that loneliness is often caused by loss. It may be loss of a partner, a job, of sight or of hearing or of mobility, even of a driving licence. The loss of someone or something which has been a central plank of your existence, of your identity, even if you didn't realise it at the time. And in its place there is that vacuum we call loneliness. And it can be very hard, usually impossible, to replace whatever or whomever you have lost. But you can get used to it and, as the queen told me, move on.

Lumley, Dame Joanna

She is beautiful, has a sultry sexy voice, is exceptionally bright and very funny. And my late husband fancied her like mad. Do I therefore hate her? Of course not. Nobody does.

I used to dream that one day I could learn her secret of lovability and copy her. Sadly I've decided that's beyond us mere mortals. In order to be like Dame Joanna, you have to look, sound, think and act like Dame Joanna. But good to have a dream.

Lunch

There are dinner people, but that's too late for me, I get hungry early. And there are lunch people: count me in. King Charles doesn't have lunch. His loss, I think. It's such a fun, attractive meal, and the Europeans have invented the siesta afterwards. Perfect.

Memorial Services

Funerals, as I have mentioned, are tough. But memorial services are far easier, because they are not just mourning a loss, and therefore heartbreaking; they are also celebrations of a life. And they should also be a reflection of your character, because the best gift you can leave your friends and family is a running order for your ideal memorial service. You will probably find you change your mind several times before you die, if you are lucky enough to live a long, full life. But it is quite fun to think through the readings and the music you would like to share as the final event of your life.

One of the best memorial services I ever attended was for Russell Harty, where the eulogy was by Alan Bennett. He told wonderful stories about Russell, which made us all laugh, and then launched a justified attack on the way the press treated him at the end of his life, saying that the 'gutter press finished him off' by hounding him,

My A–Z of surviving almost everything

disguising themselves as doctors in his hospital, mounting long lenses in the window of a flat overlooking his ward. The address was so brilliant that it was reprinted verbatim in *The Listener*.

However, since most of us can't commission Alan Bennett to do the same for us, we can always ask for Shakespeare, or John Donne, or Wendy Cope to be included. They are always worth listening to.

Men

Firstly, let me put my cards on the table. As the film *Pride* pointed out, I am binary, and I like men. (I went to a screening of *Pride*, the lovely film about the gay support for the miners' strike, and was relaxed and enjoying it when there was a scene in a van where there was a discussion about whether all women are lesbian, or at least a bit lesbian. One of the men said that's not true. A woman challenged him to name one woman who isn't lesbian and to my surprise he said 'Esther Rantzen'. He won the argument, and I agreed with him.)

Secondly, I don't believe, as some feminists seem to think, that men are always villains and women are always the victims of their villainy.

Thirdly, some men are horrible, but then some women are too.

So if you work with men, fall in love with men, vote for men, and give birth to boys, how can you distinguish between good and bad men, and make sure that your friendships and relationships are with the best ones? Always be suspicious of charm. My sister, who says many wise things, once warned me about charm. Some people, she said, use charm as a weapon. And it can be a very dangerous weapon if, like me, you are attracted to charming men. If he makes you laugh, makes you feel that you are fiercely intelligent and wildly gorgeous, beware. He is manipulating you.

However, if he looks brutal, smells horrible, and bullies and dominates you, also beware. He may tempt you into feeling sorry for him and thinking you can change him. You can't. If his mother couldn't, you won't be able to. I suggest that you keep your antennae in receive mode and take your time. After a while the hard surface will emerge through the velvety charm, and his real motives will reveal themselves.

Mice

Sweet little things. Although not when you take a bite out of a biscuit and find someone, or something, has been there before you. Which happened to me before a cat adopted us. I have sat in my favourite armchair and watched a mouse scoot across the carpet and slide under the door with his little feet sticking out behind him. Sweet little things.

Money

I was brought up by parents who believed that talking about sex, food and money was vulgar and shouldn't be done. Fashions have changed. Now it's quite difficult to talk about, or watch television programmes about, anything else. I can understand the allure of sex, and of food. But the addiction some people feel for money is odd.

Yes, we are lucky if we have the minimum we need to keep ourselves and our families warm, nourished and amused. So I realise as an ex-TV fat cat that I have been very lucky. But there are many who are way richer than I ever was, and watching them I am mystified by their quest for the biggest yacht, or the hugest hotel suite, or the youngest, sexiest wife that money can buy. Although we all love the stories about the meanness of billionaires, that doesn't seem to lead to happiness, does it? The way they flog themselves on, because enough is never enough, is very unappealing.

I've seen this close-up. I have friends and acquaintances who need to be paid a fortune so that they have the psychological status they demand. I have shared a jungle with a couple of footballers' WAGs who compared notes about how difficult it was for them to find friends who would help them decide between one designer watch and another. But personally I have never seen someone really rich with a possession or a lifestyle I envied. Not even a Picasso or an island in the Caribbean.

It's not entirely sour grapes on my part, because I almost had the chance to join these plutocrats. In 1976 I was offered a million pounds a year to transfer from the BBC to a nightly current affairs programme on ITV. Those were the days when a million pounds was a million pounds. At the time, *That's Life!*, my consumer show on BBC1, was riding high, and I couldn't abandon it, so I turned the offer down. If you want to know what it feels like to turn down a million pounds and you've never done it, it feels very stupid. What I wished in retrospect was that I had asked them to bring the dosh in a suitcase so I could have a look at it, count it, and then turn it down. That would have been fun.

When there was a scandal about unequal pay, I was asked by the lovely Fi Glover and Jane Garvey on their podcast whether I was given equal pay with men at that time, and I said absolutely not. So they said, was I paid much less? I said no, much more. And that was briefly true.

So maybe I should shut up about how unimportant money is.

M

Morning

There are owls and larks. When I was a student faced with essay deadlines, I could never write at night: I always had to get up at dawn. These days dawn has retreated to about 9am but I still prefer to work then, rather than at midnight. I have one daughter who rises with the sun and another who can't spit out a civil word before noon. They've been like that since birth. So my advice is, owl or lark, go with the flow. Don't try to fight it. It's in your DNA.

Mothers

As I have mentioned, a mother's place is in the wrong. When your kids are teenagers, they find it useful to have someone with a built-in guilt complex to blame.

My A–Z of surviving almost everything

Muesli

Not to be confused with potpourri, which can look similar.

My late husband once went on a fitness kick, and hired a personal trainer. I only knew about it when I came home from work, opened our fridge and found all my favourite cheeses had been thrown out and replaced by muesli, which was new to me as a concept and did not look very tempting. So I went up to enquire what had happened and found my husband lying on the bedroom floor with a candle in his ear. He asked me to light it. I refused. He explained that it was a Hopi remedy for deafness. He'd been introduced to it by the trainer, Carole Caplin.

Carole was, at the time, a fitness adviser and stylist working with Cherie and Tony Blair, and her boyfriend was a notorious conman we had exposed over and over again on *That's Life!* – Peter Foster. Clearly neither Cherie nor Carole watched our show often enough. However, ever since from time to time I have enjoyed a bowl of muesli.

Mumbling

Oh my lord, what is happening in the theatre? Is it the effect of television? I cannot believe it's all down to my deafness. Shall we blame Marlon Brando? The mumbling that's going on, I do hope the playwright didn't labour for years on the script, because I cannot hear a word of his deathless prose. Or poetry.

Think of the training that went into Greek actors reaching to the very back of the amphitheatre. Think of the volume produced by grand old actors, like Sir Donald Wolfit. Although I did see him in Shakespeare in Regent's

Park Open Air Theatre and the amount of spit he showered the front row with was like a tempest. In fact I think it was *The Tempest*. But at least you could hear every word.

These days I just put the subtitles on every television drama I watch, due not only to the mumbling, but also to the dubbing mixer's urge to fill each scene with sound effects, birds tweeting, planes roaring away in the sky and wind blowing a gale in the trees. I'll just point out something. Whenever Dame Maggie Smith appears in anything, you can hear every word she says. And she makes it wittier and more pointed than even Julian Fellowes or Alan Bennett knew it was when they wrote it.

Music

M

We must be instinctively attuned to music even before words begin to form in our minds. Music creates mood: sadness, happiness, courage, peace. There is nothing more poignant than the last post. Nothing more fun than 'Happy Birthday'. And music is the reason one wireless programme is always voted the best in the world: *Desert Island Discs*. The music the guests select tells you so much more about them.

If you were going to pick your favourite composer, who would it be? I suspect your answer would vary according to your mood. So I suggest that you have some of your favourite pieces of music handy, just in case. Work out your own Desert Island collection, then they will be beside you when and if you need them.

Musical Theatre

Some people (including Simon Cowell I believe), loathe it. I love it. Some of my happiest days have been spent entranced by musicals. My late husband and I once used up all his air miles to fly for a weekend to New York to immerse ourselves, and saw Glenn Close in *Sunset Boulevard* and an extraordinary production of *Kiss Me, Kate*. We were lucky enough to attend the first night of *The Phantom of the Opera*. Can you imagine, not knowing the chandelier was going to fall? So we know we have been privileged. We indulged our passion, and as super-fans, we felt we had earned the right.

When I drove my children to school, I used to set them tests in the Great American musicals 1943–1961. Which of course includes *Singin' in the Rain*, *Oklahoma!*, *Guys and Dolls* and *West Side Story*. (And I would stretch the rules to include *Carmen Jones*, because the film was released in 1954, even though Oscar Hammerstein created the book and lyric to Bizet's opera in 1943. Though sadly not *Cabaret* because that was produced in 1966, but in any case was a little too dark for my children to sing in the car.)

Anyway, I insisted then and insist now that they knew all the words. Which I have been singing since I practised being Dorothy Dandridge, running up and down the school playing fields with my hockey stick.

I once went to a charity preview of *The Lion King* and found myself sitting next to the lovely Tim Rice. I guessed he had already seen it once or twice because the moment the lights went down his eyes closed. He woke at the interval and said to me, 'Don't put your money in this, it'll take you three years to earn it back. Put your money in *Mamma Mia!* But there's quite a good song in the second half,' and fell asleep again. There was. He won an Oscar for it.

So the game I love to play these days is: which are your top ten musicals? I warn you, it can lead to bloodshed. Especially if you don't include *Cabaret*.

M

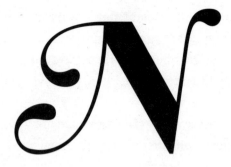

Nannies

They used to say the Battle of Waterloo was won on the play-ing fields of Eton. I say that the glorious conscientiousness of the British was drummed into them by nannies in the nurseries. Let me explain. We have just lost a head of state who ate her cereal out of Tupperware and whose favourite treat was a midge-infested barbecue in the rain. I have no criticism of Louis XIV, but there is no way he would have put up with either. Elizabeth II doubtless inherited a strong sense of duty from her father, but self-restraint? It must be in no small part down to her strict Scottish nanny, Crawfie.

And it's not restricted to the upper classes. Why did we queue so obediently, never barging in to pay our respects to the late queen when she passed away? Nanny taught us first come, first served. Why have these traditions eroded over the years? I blame the demise of the nanny.

I know that not all nannies were caring and fair. My own mother was scapegoated by her terrible Nanny Hefford, who singled her out for punishment and humiliation from which she was only released when her older sister Marion told my grandmother, 'Nanny is really cruel to Katherine.' And she was, as her schoolfriends testified.

But when they were good, nannies were very, very good, so that their upper-class nurselings used to run to them first, even when adults, to tell them the good news of their engagement, or seek help over something of concern or distress. Not surprising, since it's astonishing that aristocratic parents ever recognised their own children. They were sent away to boarding school from the age of seven (or even earlier) and were not seen again until they came into their inheritance. It was Winston Churchill's nanny who alerted his mother to the brutal beating he was suffering at school and insisted that he must be taken away. Good on you, nanny.

So when politicians call us a nanny state, I take that as a compliment. Firm but fair.

Naps

How good are they? After a good lunch, in front of the television, as your eyelids gently close together. A nap is contented, it's refreshing, and it sets you up for a happy afternoon. One of the great discoveries of growing older. I thoroughly recommend it.

National Treasures

During my career I have progressed through many different labels. 'Toothy Esther Rantzen' was the first one. That lasted even after my large teeth got fixed; journalists are often not very observant. But my labels then evolved into 'Veteran

Esther Rantzen', and occasionally 'An Institution', which made me feel like an old psychiatric hospital. And now, when someone is feeling affectionate, I am one of the many people called 'National Treasures'. Which is extremely flattering, but not a phrase I would use about others.

For instance, one we all agree about is Dame Judi Dench. 'National Treasure' is just inadequate to sum up what we owe her for her extraordinary artistry over the years. Take just one example, her Oscar-winning eight-minute performance as Elizabeth I in *Shakespeare in Love*. She managed to sum up authority, the battle involved in being a woman in a man's world, the harsh requirements of tradition, and a love of the theatre, all contained in hardly any words, and a tiny part. Who else could do that?

So if they really are talents that the nation does treasure, that phrase doesn't do their uniqueness anything like proper credit.

Nepotism

This can be an extremely bad idea, but occasionally is a surprisingly good one. Are we against the accession of George VI to the throne to succeed his abdicating brother? Divine right is obvious nepotism, and in this case it saved the monarchy.

Are we against the Dimbleby brothers achieving huge success in the broadcast media excelled in by their late father, Richard? Obviously not – just a case of inherited talent.

However, not too enthusiastic about Kim Jong-Un, son of Kim Jong-Il, both rulers of North Korea and obviously owing their terrifying supremacy to nepotism. So in that case extremely dangerous.

Though I must admit my father worked for the BBC before I did, as a leading engineer, but in fact had small regard for programme makers. So maybe in our case it was not nepotism, I hope. Though since he was the reason I thought the BBC would be a fascinating place to work, it was certainly networking (see *Networking*).

Networking

It can be incredibly productive to bring different worlds together to create something new. I remember being invited by Barnado's to attend a lunch honouring children of courage. It was such a moving occasion that when Mark Patterson, the producer of *Children in Need*, rang me to ask if I had an idea for a programme during Pudsey's evening that would give Terry Wogan the chance to refresh, I came up with the television version: *Children of Courage*, which ran for years and moved and inspired viewers.

(In fact it was only killed by the first example of extreme wokeness, a disabled lobby who claimed it was 'patronising'. Yes, some of the children had disabilities, but not all; what united them all was their courage and their altruism. All of them brought donations to help other children. Typical wokery revealing itself to be bigotry, and in nobody's interests. One of my disabled friends said to me, 'Are disabled people the only ones not allowed to receive awards?')

The 'satire boom' on television was created by bringing the current affairs department and entertainment talents together. I got my job there because I had met some of the satire team when I was at university, a very happy example of networking in my life. As is the fact that charities are often created by introducing those who have suffered to those who can donate to support them.

I never used to turn down an invitation just in case useful networking occurred. I remember once being invited to give the prizes at Kingston Hospital to nurses who had given up smoking; nurses used to be notorious for their difficulty giving up cigarettes. While I was there a consultant anaesthetist started to talk to me about a case of a toddler who had just died falling forward onto a handbrake when the car was travelling only at about ten miles an hour and the little girl was standing up in the back. He said, 'You wouldn't put your fine china loose on the back seat of the car – why put your children there?'

All around me there were people trying to interrupt us, but I wouldn't let them. I took his name and we filmed me arriving at my children's school with my children loose in the back of my car, and we quoted him. Then we showed a film shot in America of what happened in a head-on collision. The children's dummies were thrown straight through the windscreen. As a result the Minister for Transport, Peter Bottomley, agreed to commission some video made in Britain showing the same thing, and a private member's bill was put through Parliament. For me, a perfect example of the positive impact of networking.

Nudity

I'm in favour. Skinny-dipping feels lovely. The sun on your skin makes you glad all over. And if we all did it more often, everyone would accept body hair and lumps. And there might be less piercing.

My A–Z of surviving almost everything

Opulence

I am so bourgeoise and middle class that if it's flashy, I feel uncomfortable. I'd rather be cosy. But I do realise that some people really get the taste for opulence, especially if they have experienced poverty in their youth. I sometimes wonder why I am so contented in a cottage when friends of mine demand mansions, but at least it means I'm not in thrall to envy, the most destructive emotion of all (see *Jealousy*).

Organisations

When Childline was very new, I went on holiday to the Galapagos Islands, in a group which included several psychiatrists from Florida. I told one of them about Childline, and how challenging it was to meet the enormous demand we had uncovered (50,000 attempted calls on the first night Childline opened) and that some of our team were creating new rules for no obvious rhyme or reason, and he said, 'On day one, an organisation's aim is to help its customers. From day two, its aim is to protect itself.'

This has been true of every organisation I've ever worked with, even charities. Especially charities. It's a constant challenge to remember and remind everyone else, especially those in middle management, that their job is to provide the service the customers need, not to protect the organisation. Because if you try to protect the organisation at the expense of the customer, it will rebound back anyway. Watching the muddles the BBC gets into, nine times out of ten it's when somebody decides to protect the organisation instead of the viewers or listeners. It's the same with Boris. It's the same with the Post Office. It's the same with the Church. It's the same with ... well, you fill in the blanks. I'm sure you've come across it as often as I have.

O

My A–Z of surviving almost everything

Paparazzi

I had the doubtful privilege of interviewing some of these ruthless, heartless photographers who were blithely unashamed about their motive: money. They told me that a picture of Princess Diana smiling and looking beautiful was valueless to them – there were thousands of those. They needed a shot of her in tears, or hiding her face, something obviously unhappy which could be worth £250,000 worldwide. So they would use any method, calling her terrible names, pursuing her against her will; nothing was too cruel or vicious.

One told me of the occasion when the princess's father had just died, and she was in a hotel on the ski slopes when she was told the news. So she ran out onto a terrace to be alone, heard the click of a long lens, looked up and cried, 'Oh no, not here!' and he got the picture he needed.

There is no doubt in my mind that they pursued Diana to her death. The recent documentaries by Harry and

Meghan describe the same hunters surrounding them, too. I have never forgotten a curator at a zoo explaining that unless you give an animal some privacy, especially with their mates and their young, they will go mad. Interestingly, the internet has just disgorged trolls who rival paparazzi in their nastiness. So far, nobody has discovered an effective shield from them.

Parenting

Odd, isn't it, that a skill on which the survival of our species depends, in a role that can happen, often does happen, accidentally, and for which there are no qualifications, can differ so widely historically and geographically.

Remember how they used to swaddle babies in medieval times? According to my daughter, swaddling has come back into fashion, though I can't believe it's good for babies.

Remember 'spare the rod and spoil the child', so beloved of Victorian schoolmasters? When I demand-fed my babies I was warned, not by a schoolmaster but a maternity nurse, that was what I was doing.

My mother never approved of demand feeding. She used to leave me and my sister crying in our pram in the garden until the clock said it was mealtime, even though, in my sister's case as she was born in February, that meant the baby crying while snow was falling on the pram, and perhaps on the baby too. But she survived. Thankfully.

As children we both survived the era of the rod, and when we were mothers in our turn it was the age of the naughty step. Once, when my six-year-old son had flung a marble egg dangerously close to the television set which could have exploded all over him, I took his chubby little hand, unfolded the fingers, smacked the palm, and explained that was so that he would remember the rule about not throwing anything indoors in future. He drew himself up to his full height, walked in a stately and dignified way out of the door, and went and sat on the stairs, where I found him. 'Let's have a hug,' I said to him, trying not to make myself sound pleading. 'Not until you say sorry,' he said, clearly in command of the high moral ground. 'I'm very sorry I had to smack your hand,' I said, and he relented enough to hug me. But I'm not sure either corporal punishment or the naughty step put this parent in charge of that encounter.

Parenting is an obstacle course. Somehow you have to surmount each new challenge: the nappies, the temper tantrums, the schools, sex education, religion, bullying – there's a new test around every corner. Probably several new ones. And then when they're old enough to have to face these challenges themselves, they blame you for any difficulties they face as adults. 'It's your fault, Mum – how can anything compare with the holidays we had as children?' one of them told me. 'You were at work so much no wonder I have separation fears,' said another. A mother's place, as I may have mentioned, is in the wrong (see *Mothers* and *Happiness*).

Parties

I went to a marvellous party, said Noel Coward, and it's true: when a party is marvellous, it really is marvellous. It all depends upon the host. Firstly, there needs to be food as well as drink, otherwise people get squiffy and start shouting at each other and nobody can hear anything. Then there need to be introductions. So somebody needs to know everyone, and be able to guess who will enjoy meeting whom. Also, it helps to have something to do, like a band to listen to, or a bouncy castle to jump on, or fancy dress to be embarrassed by.

Above all, pick your guests with care, because nobody wants to get stuck with a bore. Although if you happen to be a bore yourself, that won't matter because you can grab a plate of sausage rolls and take them around as you introduce people to each other, and nobody will be stuck with you.

Perks

Some perks are worth having, but not all. When I worked in a BBC building, the Lime Grove Studios, I didn't have a car park pass, and I had to park my car miles away, which was a nuisance in bad weather. So one day I examined the bosses' cars parked in the small car park, memorised what their passes looked like, and then went back to my office, drew one and stuck it in my windscreen. From then on they let me park there.

A few weeks later the premises manager rang me up and asked if I would take it down because the commissionaires knew it was a fake but were too embarrassed to stop me. I saw his point. However, at about the same time a double-glazing salesman rang the BBC and said if I carried on spoiling his business by exposing door-to-door salesmen on *That's Life!* he knew where I worked and when I arrived there he'd be waiting for me to punch my famous teeth down my throat. The bosses got worried and

P

gave me an official car park pass. And before you ask, no, it wasn't me ringing the BBC and pretending to be the angry salesman. It was a real one.

I imagine the bosses who also parked there were irritated, because perks are a very important part of being a boss. How else do they know they are important? When Desmond became a head of department someone from HR came and explained that now he was eligible for full-draw curtains and a cocktail cabinet in his office. When David Attenborough became controller of BBC2 he told Desmond that as an experiment he put a bottle of Malvern water on his desk with two glasses and waited to see how long it would take for the other controllers with offices in the same corridor to copy. It took a week. Status is very competitive.

And of course, if you book a major star for your feature film or your festival, they always have riders on their contract to prove their status. For example, a dressing room painted lilac. Or boxes of Smarties with all the blue ones removed.

P

I was accused by a rather sour executive producer of the series *Hearts of Gold* of exerting privilege by not allowing anyone to sit next to me at the final script session. In fact, it was so that our wonderful make-up lady, Anabela, could sit there and paint my nails while we were working on the script, on the grounds that if she did it any earlier in the day I was so klutzy that I would chip them and she'd have to start over. But maybe he was also right, that it was a perk to have her paint my nails instead of doing them myself.

The trouble with perks is that if you've got them you do tend to take them for granted. Rich, powerful people aren't necessarily the best company.

Pets

There is a price for everything. In return for companionship you have a responsibility to pick up after them, and make sure they are happily looked after if you go away. Also they may have a shorter life than you have, which means heartbreak if they pass away.

It's always been my ambition to have a pet pig. They are so engaging, and obviously intelligent. I'm not sure if you can house-train them, though.

Piercings

Yuck.

Playpens

Whatever happened to them? A brilliant refuge for a toddler, you could fling their favourite toys into the middle and be sure they wouldn't wander over to open the cupboards of bleach or play with the biggest kitchen knives. Then, for some reason, playpens went out of style. Why?

P

My A–Z of surviving almost everything

Podcasts

What fun they are. Or some of them are. Others are so dull they send you into deep sleep (see *Insomnia*). Both have their uses. But as a professional producer it fascinates me that podcasts, which are often self-produced, can be so much more interesting than carefully crafted programmes. I think that's because professional producers are too impatient. Any thought that rambles a little or an idea that spreads longer than two minutes they edit ruthlessly. And that's a mistake.

My favourite podcast is *The Rest Is Politics*, which is a series of topical conversations between Alastair Campbell and Rory Stewart. They come from opposite ends of the political spectrum but manage to have civilised conversations about the news of the week, shining a light on it from the world they both have lived and worked in for years.

I recommend you explore podcasts when you have a moment to yourself, you will not regret it.

P

Politeness (and Punctuality)

It is said that punctuality is the politeness of princes. Both are useful ways of showing that you care about others' feelings without encouraging unwelcome familiarity.

Politicians

Some of my best friends have become politicians. I think it's dangerous to write them all off, as some journalists do, as dishonest, or untruthful or corrupt. We have to be alert in case they are, but dismissing them all is unfair. We need to respect them, but not revere them.

For instance, Jack Ashley was a great politician, supporting and drawing attention to very important causes, like the thalidomide scandal. And speaking personally I admired Margaret Thatcher, known as the 'Iron Lady', although I did not always agree with her. She genuinely cared about protecting children from harm, which is why when she was prime minister she gave Childline a reception at 10 Downing Street, in the charity's earliest days. A memory I will share with you because it shows a different side to her, as well as her consummate political skill.

The Downing Street reception really put Childline on the map. Mrs T made sure that all the ministers with any responsibility for vulnerable children attended to hear about the brand new charity, as did rich and famous potential donors and supporters, so it was a very crucial event in Childline's history. I remember standing next to the prime minister in front of the famous Downing Street fireplace, shaking hands with the great and the good as they arrived, and pinching myself with disbelief that I was there.

P

When there was a lull between arrivals, Mrs T turned to me and said, 'Miss Rantzen, what are the long-term effects of child abuse?'

'Well, Prime Minister,' I said, 'if everything we learn about love and trust and loyalty we learn from our own parents, and if instead we learn about pain, and fear, and shame, it's no wonder that so many abuse victims end up in addiction units, and prisons, with failed marriages or living rough on the streets.'

By this time her famous blue eyes had glazed, and I thought, 'Terrific. I've bored my family for forty years,

I've bored television audiences by the million and now I've bored the prime minister.' Then guests started to arrive again, and we continued to shake hands and pose for photographs.

When the time came for Mrs Thatcher to speak, she got onto a little embroidered footstool so everyone could see her and started to talk about Christmas and the NSPCC, which she supported. Then she said, 'You know, when we consider the long-term effects of child abuse, if everything we learn about love, and trust, and loyalty we learn from our own parents, and if instead we learn about pain, and fear, and shame ...'

And I thought two things. Firstly, thank heavens that was not my speech, because I was speaking second. And secondly, she certainly takes a brief brilliantly. Because without realising it, that was what I had done; I had briefed her, and that must have been how she survived Prime Minister's Questions so well. She recognised the quote she could use, and the right moment to use it.

She finished her speech, introduced me, and I climbed onto the little stool and read every word of my speech, absolutely terrified of the challenge, of having this one chance to explain to the most influential audience in Britain why Childline was so crucial and must be supported. It was not possible to bring children or young people into the reception, so it was a huge responsibility to try to explain why they found it impossible to ask for help any other way, and why Childline would play a unique role in protecting them.

When I finished, the third speaker was a volunteer fundraiser. She said, 'My father was a policeman and a

Freemason, and I tell you that because I want you to know how respected he was in our village. But nobody knew what happened in our home when the front door had shut behind him ...' Then she burst into tears. And in that moment, the audience in that state room, with its gold-striped wallpaper and glittering chandeliers, heard the voice of the abused child.

She got off the stool, and I got onto it in her place and explained that she was fundraising for Childline because she knew that although she could not rescue yesterday's children like herself, she could protect today's children, like her own, and tomorrow's. Then I looked around for her and someone told me she was in the prime minister's study.

So I went there, a comfortable room with a sofa where our fundraiser was sitting while the prime minister bustled around fetching her a towel and filling a glass of water for her, saying, 'Don't try to stop yourself crying, my dear; it's far better not to try to bottle up your emotion. You will be quite private here, stay as long as you like, nobody will disturb you.'

I thought to myself, is this really the Iron Lady? So obviously compassionate, doing and saying exactly the right thing? I said, 'I'll stay with her, Prime Minister, if you would like to go back to the party.' And she left.

But that was not the end of the story. Because on the way home Desi stopped to buy an evening paper, and the banner headline on the front page read ABUSE VICTIM SOBS IN NUMBER TEN. 'The prime minister held a reception today for the children's helpline Childline and comforted an abuse victim who ...' So her excellent press team had seen what I saw, the compassionate side to the Iron Lady. And the news story they put out did her good, but also of course did Childline good. It was definitely win-win.

Now, I think that story illustrates what politicians can do to support a good cause and be professional themselves. And that's why I don't belong to the Paxman view that they are all liars and need to be exposed. I think they have great potential to do good, most of them. Though of course we have to be alert because not all of them should be trusted. Which is true of every profession, isn't it?

The last time I met Mrs Thatcher it was at an event where she had been advised not to speak, but did, perfectly well. By then she had already suffered a few strokes and was rumoured to be a bit doolally. I went up to her and introduced myself and said, 'Lady Thatcher, thank you so much for supporting Childline in our earliest days. You made a huge difference.' She looked at me with those blue eyes I remembered so well and said, 'Nothing is more important than protecting children from abuse. Nothing.' And I thought, if you're doolally, I want to go doolally like that.

The moral of that story, I suppose, is that whether you agree with a politician or not, they may still earn your respect.

Pop Songs

'A, You're Adorable'. They don't write songs like that any more. They were written by professional songwriters, for one thing, and they had tunes and rhymes and metres, and sold millions of records. For some reason the songs that were popular around 1948-49 stuck in my childish memory and stick there still. I can warble several choruses of 'Candy Kisses' and 'Red Roses for a Blue Lady'. But there is no doubt in my mind that pop songs only really burst into bloom with the Beatles.

It was *Sgt. Pepper*, of course, that changed everything. Or at least changed our expectations, even if nothing else could compare.

Pornography

Abusive and exploitative, a horrible industry about which, I admit, I am no expert. Although one of my first tasks as a reporter on the consumer programme *Braden's Week* was to investigate male escorts. For some reason this took me into one of the sex shops in Soho where I remember asking a shopkeeper if he knew any nice men to take me out to dinner, while averting my eyes from unflattering black-and-white stills of blow jobs. He was polite but unhelpful, and obviously mystified by my persistence. I did eventually find a young man who took me out, brought me home, and knew one of my uncles on the stock exchange. But in those dear, dead days pornography was quite difficult to access. Now, of course, thanks to the internet, the average age that a child first watches pornography is ten. Is that progress? I think not.

Pregnancy

Is it old-fashioned, possibly illegal in Scotland, to suggest that only a woman can be pregnant? I look back on the state of pregnancy as strange but wondrous. My first symptom was a metallic taste in my mouth and the fact that tea, coffee and alcohol were suddenly totally undrinkable. I gather all three are bad for growing embryos. My second

P

symptom was morning sickness, and as I was trying to keep the pregnancies secret for the first three months, I remember throwing up on my way to work, leaning over the wall of a local cemetery hoping nobody would notice. My third symptom for the second and third pregnancies were growing to the size of a barn. A large barn. I once co-presented Miss World when I was hugely pregnant. That was a peculiar professional moment.

Anyway, for anyone who hasn't experienced it, I recommend it. It's a unique moment, lying in the bath watching lumps in your own abdomen moving as the baby inside kicks and pushes independently in ways completely out of your control. Which is how she will doubtless continue for the rest of her life.

Prince Philip, Duke of Edinburgh

When you consider the famously successful marriage of Philip and Elizabeth, two assets spring to mind: humour and tolerance. Obviously they fancied each other; he was outstandingly handsome and she was pretty and shy and had a job for life. So you can see why they married, in spite of the opposition from the snobs who said he wasn't good enough. But why did they stay married? Humour and tolerance.

Princess Anne

I've seen her at various events, and when she makes a speech she never relies upon notes; she's a clever lady. When she was young she had the reputation of being very blunt, like her father, telling photographers to Naff

Orf. And you can understand why. It's rare to see a good photograph of her, because she's normally in profile, and that's not her best angle. She has clearly never been vain enough to study the angles, and stand and smile slightly more full face, to ensure the pictures are more flattering.

I was instructed in this by Anton du Beke, the ballroom dancer turned television judge. He had the misfortune of dancing with me in series two of *Strictly*, fortunately expunged from most people's memory, not mine, and perhaps not his, given the number of times I trod on him. Anyway, the trick is this. Stand as tall as you can but lower your chin. Pull the stomach in to touch the spine. Drop one hip. Women, put one hand on the hip you have dropped. Smile. Men, place one hand in a pocket. Smile.

The last time I met Princess Anne was when she presented me with my damehood. She pinned the sharp, shiny brooch onto my dress at the waist, then said, 'Be careful, you can do yourself serious damage with this when you sit down.' Which turned out to be true. Then she asked me about Childline and The Silver Line and said the challenge is to create trust. Which is also absolutely true.

Princesses

Interesting: the small girls in my life all want to dress as princesses with pink net and sparkles, and none of the small boys would dream of dressing as princes.

Programmes

The more choice you have, the less television you want to view. Discuss.

Putin

Revealed to be a monster. Sometimes I think extinction is the only answer to human ferocity.

Puzzles

Fun. I prefer word games. Some love jigsaws or sudoku. Whatever your choice, they are all excellent ways to challenge the brain.

The Queen

As Joni Mitchell says in 'Big Yellow Taxi', you don't know what you've got until it's gone. For decades we took the queen for granted. By comparison with Princess Diana, let's admit it, the rest of the royal family, including the queen, seemed rather old-fashioned and dull. Then in 1997 when Diana tragically died, and nobody flew a flag at half-mast over Buckingham Palace, public anger grew because it looked as if rules and protocol were crushing the nation's need to offer respect and compassion. But as the years went by, perhaps we learned to appreciate the queen more; perhaps she herself changed.

And yet Queen Elizabeth was always very careful to abide by the rule book for a constitutional monarch. Say very little. If you have to speak, stay away from anything too personal or controversial. Never express your own political views. Wear the same shoes and carry the same handbag for decades. She also stuck with the same breeds of dogs, her corgis and dorgis, wore matching coats and hats and a hairstyle that stoutly withstood fashion and headscarves. So what does this teach us, given her extraordinary survival? That progress should be gradual, that dullness is a virtue.

But was she really as dull as she seemed? Perhaps it was crucial to the role, as she saw it, especially as she and her family worked to reconstruct the family firm that had been shaken to its foundations by the abdication of Edward VIII, a glamorous figure until he gave up the job, and the challenges of World War II.

I don't know about you, but I find I can remember events of 70 years ago far more vividly than what happened last week, or even this morning. So I remember the last time we had a king, George VI. When I was very young, my family used to listen to every royal Christmas message, broadcast by the king at 3pm on Christmas Day, on the wireless. And when the national anthem played, we stood to attention in our sitting room. So I was brought up to sing 'God Save Our Gracious King'.

My mother used to tell me how badly the king had been treated, made to talk with pebbles in his mouth to cure his stammer, which of course it didn't. She was an ardent monarchist, told me how brave the king and queen were during the war, refusing to move out of Buckingham Palace and visiting the East End when they had been bombed to smithereens in the Blitz. She was shocked when he died, although she said how terribly gaunt and ill he had looked when he saw Elizabeth and Philip off at the airport. And then suddenly we had a queen as head of state for the first time since Victoria.

Queen Elizabeth II was so young, and so serious as she navigated her way through the complications of the coronation. Soon afterwards, in 1953, she came to our local town hall and we were given the day off school to go and wave small Union Jacks, and I well remember being thrilled to see her drive past us wearing a pretty flowered hat, but I never thought I'd meet her. However, I did. And naturally I treasure the memories.

I first met Her Majesty the Queen at a party at BAFTA, the British Academy of Film and Television Arts, in Piccadilly. I remember seeing her walk straight towards me looking exactly like a stamp, or a penny, and it felt surreal because her image was so familiar. At the time I was presenting the TV consumer programme *That's Life!* and she obviously watched it, because she said to me, 'Don't you find it depressing, telling all those stories of people being cheated?' And I said, 'No, Your Majesty, because they want us to tell their stories to protect other people from being cheated too.' I suspect one reason she watched a consumer programme like ours was to stay in touch with what her subjects were experiencing.

Q

The queen presented me with my OBE for services to broadcasting. But she didn't talk to me about television. Instead, she said to me, 'Are you still involved with Childline?' which had just been launched. When I said I was, she asked how our volunteers and staff coped with listening to so many children talking about their suffering, and I said that once we had listened and reassured them that their suffering was not their fault, and that they could be protected, the children felt far more confident and hopeful. Finally she held out her hand to shake mine, said

'Goodbye' and pushed me vigorously straight backwards into the obligatory curtsey. Because of course you mustn't turn your back on the queen. Now I mention that because it might be a useful technique when trying to get rid of a door-to-door salesman, or a guest who outstays their welcome. The push, as I recall, needs to be quite vigorous.

Incidentally, there's another tip I learned from Prime Minister Margaret Thatcher, who held a reception for Childline in Number 10, and whom I stood next to in the receiving line. As each guest arrived, she took their hand, paused so they could be photographed shaking hands, and then firmly moved their hand and hers from left to right, forcing them to move along. Very useful at weddings and bar mitzvahs.

The last time I met Her Majesty was on a very hot day at St James's Palace in 2012, at an event to celebrate the work of volunteers. She arrived unexpectedly, wearing a blue-and-white dress with a big diamond brooch, looking as fresh as a daisy when we were all wilting in the heat – no air conditioning in St James's Palace. She came over to my group and said to me, 'Why are you here?' I explained that it was probably because Childline's service is delivered by volunteers, and due to once again being overawed and my brain unravelling – I expect she frequently has this effect on people, so she must be used to it – I carried on. '... And now, you'll probably think I'm mad, I'm thinking of starting up a similar helpline for older people who are lonely and vulnerable.' She looked into the distance, with a slightly grumpy expression, and I wondered whether I'd said something wrong, but then I realised she was thinking. We don't often see the queen thinking because usually she is either smiling and waving or reading a speech. Then she said, 'I suppose some of the problems older people face are the same as the ones that children face.' I said, 'Yes, Your Majesty, especially since neglect or abuse is often carried out by the people who should love and care for them.' She looked into the distance again, once again with that grumpy expression which I now realised meant she was reflecting on our conversation, then she said, 'Well, I don't think it's mad, I think it's rather brave.' I was thrilled, rushed back to tell our Silver Line trustees, and it gave us the courage to keep calm and carry on.

I don't think enough credit is given to the difference the royal family make to the voluntary sector. When they attend charity events, everyone crowds in, including the rich potential donors charities rely upon. The press and TV arrive, so charities can spread awareness of their work. They make a huge difference. And the trustees and I were definitely heartened when the queen reassured us that we weren't mad, we were rather brave in creating The Silver Line helpline. So, as Paddington Bear memorably said to her: Thank you, for everything.

Would the queen have dared to have tea with Paddington, or jump from a helicopter with James Bond at the start of her reign? Certainly not. She would have been harshly judged, blamed for not taking the job seriously enough. Could she, by the end of her reign? Absolutely. She'd earned the right to have fun. I think all older people have the right to have fun. And I'm saddened by the number of callers to The Silver Line helpline for isolated older people who tell us that it's been decades since they had fun. Or that fun is just for young people. No it's not.

Ask Paddington.

Queues

Some nations excel in industry, some in democracy, some in baseball, some in chess. England pioneered sports such as cricket, football and rugby, and exported them so successfully that other nations adopted them and even outclassed British teams, rather meanly. But in one skill Britain still rules the world, and that is in queueing.

We queue with passion. Television's second most favourite couple, Phil Schofield and Holly Willoughby from ITV's *This Morning*, were invulnerable, Teflon to any criticism until they were accused of queue-jumping when the late queen was lying in state. Blasphemy. The British do not queue-jump.

Foreigners do try to emulate our skill. Disney, when they created their Disneylands and Worlds, elevated queue control to an art form by snaking the lines back and forth so that nobody could quite work out how long it really was. Other nations do things differently. In Israel you are expected to join a queue where a friend has already staked a good position. It is said that in the United Arab Emirates the rulers are expected to go straight to the front without waiting. That would bring about a revolution in Britain. Why are we so obedient to the first come, first served rule?

Perhaps it is true that the British have an innate sense of fairness. It may not always be applied and there are plenty of cases of injustice that need righting, but the instinct is still there. And our national skill in queueing even when only two people are waiting bears witness to it.

Quizzes

So helpful. I'm sure you have blind spots, as I do, and the way our temperamental memories sometimes disgorge facts from long ago but at other moments refuse to offer any suggestions at all, especially about this morning or last week, can be very disconcerting. So watching quizzes, and being occasionally reassured by the obscure facts you can disinter and shout at the screen, is great fun. Fortunately, quizzes are so universally popular that the gods who rule television schedules may allow us to continue to enjoy them. May.

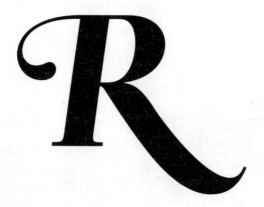

Reality TV

If the term means extracting entertainment from real people, blame me. Because the programme *That's Life!* was a pioneer, with our street interviews and our talent contests, and amateur musicians playing everything, from watering cans and each other's skulls to false teeth and cow clusters. But the current trend of creating competitions in every field, from sex to murder, using ordinary people as the contestants, is taking the genre to a new high. Or low. Fine, if you enjoy watching and they enjoy playing. Not so fine if they get horribly trolled by social media.

Recruitment

Two friends of mine used to divide humanity into those with grasp and those with flair. And it is sometimes helpful to make that distinction, because in my experience both types of personality benefit from working with each other.

Personally, I would put the flair in charge, because they are good at vision and empathy, and the grasp as a strong deputy, running the budget and getting the detail right. My view of Boris, feel free to differ, is that if only he'd had a strong deputy he would allow to advise him, he could have done the right thing by Ukraine and the vaccine roll-out, without losing everyone's confidence by enabling drunken parties in Number 10 when they were forbidden and appointing dodgy politicians.

My advice, when recruiting, is not to trust interviews: they are notoriously unreliable. Give candidates appropriate tests. And never rely on management consultants. They are the vultures of the professions, perched on the boss's shoulder as they peck the vulnerable, put in an incomprehensible structure and fly away before they are found out. That's my experience, anyway.

My A–Z of surviving almost everything

Relatives

Very good training for your tolerance. But bear in mind, as you grow older, that the ones who are younger than you are probably the ones who are going to choose your nursing home, so keep them on side if you can.

Rows

Malcolm Muggeridge, once the editor of *Punch* and in later years known as 'the Sage of Robertsbridge', used to say, 'The row is never about the row.' And there is truth in that. Very often the row is not about the thing you or they did wrong; it's about the attempt to cover it up. Sometimes the row is about something tactless someone said.

A cousin of mine got married and didn't invite me. Then his sister told me what a lovely occasion it had been, and how surprised the other guests were that I wasn't there. Which resulted in years of family *broigus*.

Broigus is a wonderful Yiddish word for a feud, or a bitter dispute. It comes from the Yiddish because, and as a Jew myself I hope you will forgive me boasting, Jews do *broigus* better than anyone. I once spoke at a Jewish charity lunch and one couple walked out even before the starters were served, because they disapproved of the table plan. Many people have walked out while I'm making a speech, but few do it before the starter. That was a terrific example of *broigus*.

And while I'm on the subject of weddings and table plans, let me offer another piece of advice. Forget the table plan. You never know in advance who would love to sit next to who, who grew up together and would love to catch up again, who loathes whose guts.

I tried to persuade my daughter not to have a table plan when she was having her wedding blessed in our garden, but she resisted me and said she had to have a plan. It was expected. So we compromised. We worked out what table each guest would sit at but let them decide themselves exactly who they'd sit next to.

One of the best hostesses I have ever met has a different solution. She gives the most wonderful dinners, with dozens of guests, and on arrival each one is handed a numbered ticket, with different colours depending whether they are men or women. (These days I suppose you might hand out rainbow ones as well, to cover all eventualities.) Anyway, you knew that it would be pure luck who you ended up next to, but as all her guests are fascinating people, you didn't care because you knew you were sure to have a fabulous time.

I suppose that wouldn't work if you have friends or family who are deadly bores, but it works brilliantly for her. For me, I would stick with guests having allocated tables, but let them choose whoever they want to sit next to. Then if it ends up in a *broigus*, it's their own fault.

R

Royal Variety Shows

I've been in two of these (formerly called Royal Command Shows). Appearing in the show is now the top prize for the winner of *Britain's Got Talent*. The first time, they staged the Ascot scene from *My Fair Lady* and I was incorporated, fortunately performing well within my limitations. I just had to walk onto the stage arm in arm with the comedian Cyril Fletcher, who was a great friend. That was fine, and afterwards I met Princess Diana, who was in her fairy tale princess phase, with a diamond tiara and a long, sparkling blue dress the colour of her eyes. If only I'd left it at that.

Unfortunately, the second time I was asked to do more, to sing and dance in a specially choreographed routine with two other TV journalists, Jan Leeming and Gloria Hunniford, both of whom had the unfair advantage that they really sing. Anyway, I learned the dance routine painfully slowly (as I have already admitted, I discovered on *Strictly Come Dancing* that I have no muscle memory) and then the time came to go to the theatre and perform.

The sad thing was that the conductor played our music – which was the Irving Berlin song 'Anything You Can Do, I Can Do Better', from *Annie Get Your Gun* – very slowly. Now, if you are dancing or singing to a song which is playing very slowly, it means you have to stand for a long time on one leg, so you wobble, and sing for a long time on one note, which can get screechy. The song ended, eventually, and so did the show, and the Queen Mother came round backstage to meet us all and thank us.

When she reached us, she shook my hand and said, 'You must have been so relieved when that finished,' which made us realise how relieved she and the rest of the audience must have felt. The then theatre critic of the *Daily Mail*, Jack Tinker, wrote a review saying, 'Gloria Hunniford, Jan Leeming and Esther Rantzen sang, "Anything you can do (I can do better)", and proved they couldn't.'

So when the contestants in talent shows say 'follow your dream', and 'you can do anything', that's not always good advice. Hope can lead you into disaster. Either have a good friend who will dissuade you from a rash ambition or have a very revealing mirror which shows you your limitations. And don't do it unless you have the talent. Dream away, but only in your bedroom.

Rudeness

Do you remember Michael Winner, the erstwhile film director and food critic? He was renowned for his rudeness. The manager of a famous country house hotel he used to patronise told me Michael would sit in the middle of their restaurant waving a handkerchief in one hand until he had the full attention of the head waiter. And if at the last moment he rang to book their best room over a bank holiday and it was fully booked, he used to try to cajole the manager into pretending they'd had a plumbing disaster and turn other customers out so he could stay there. The manager told me that whenever Michael booked they would put a member of staff onto him the whole time he was there, to look after him because he was so much trouble. Sir Sydney Samuelson, a lovely doyen of the film industry, once told me Michael had reduced an elderly projectionist to tears. So that's who he was. Not always a rude bully, but often.

R

So when I did a talk show about rudeness, I suggested Michael as our main guest. He said he would do it if we only had one person on our podium: him. We normally had a panel. I said fine, only him.

We always recorded two programmes in a day, and the first one overran a little while we were seating the audience. Towards the end, Anabela, our make-up lady, came into the control room looking distressed and said Michael Winner had already arrived and was now threatening to walk out. I said I'd come and talk to him, because I'd met him quite often at parties, and I walked into make-up. Michael was sitting there, red in the face, bloodshot eyes, and barked at me that unless we started in less than two minutes he would walk out. So I explained that in our first programme I had interviewed a child who was a little shy, so it had taken me more time, but the audience were almost seated so we would indeed be starting in a few moments. And we did.

The title music sounded, I entered, delivered an introduction about rude people, then turned to Michael and said, 'Michael, why did you insist on being the only person on the podium?' In my earpiece I heard my editor and the cameramen all gasp, shocked by my rudeness, I imagine.

I know what happened next because Michael wrote about it in an article. He says that he had become heartily sick of broadcasters keeping him waiting, that once Professor Anthony Clare, presenter of the wonderful radio programme *In the Psychiatrist's Chair*, was delayed by a flight from Dublin, so Michael had walked out of the studio rather than waiting for him. When we were delayed, he described how he had threatened to walk out on us. He said that when we started slightly late, I had asked him that first question, and he contemplated walking out then. But he thought to himself, 'That's just the publicity the old bag wants,' so he didn't.

If only he had said that on the programme, the viewers would have been highly entertained, we would have begun with a bang and the whole show would have worked. Instead he had answered me as sweetly as a dove, thus ruining it. Although if I'd had my wits about me I could have suggested that my own question was a good example of rudeness, but I hadn't and I didn't.

So what is the moral there? Never be rude to a studio guest? Ah, if only interviewers complied with that rule, wouldn't that make much more enjoyable listening? Never invite Michael Winner to a studio debate? He has now passed on to the Almighty's debating chamber in the sky. Or perhaps to the infernal one down below; if so, that would certainly involve a sizeable amount of rudeness.

Rumours

Don't believe them. Especially conspiracy theories. In these days of alternative facts, don't believe them unless and until the evidence is there before your eyes. And still doubt then.

Seasons

Each one has its own beauty. For me, spring and early summer are heartbreakingly lovely, but then autumn leaves and winter frost also tug at your heartstrings. We are lucky if we are warm and dry enough to appreciate them. Not everyone is, of course.

Sell-by Dates

Wasteful and daft, whether applied to food or people.

Sex

Sex drives people mad. Probably that's what it's for, because if you think about it, if you were sane, would you do such an inelegant, unhygienic thing? You definitely wouldn't if you were a male praying mantis. During mating the female mantis bites his head off and then eats the rest of his body for pudding. So if he were sensible he'd avoid her and there'd be no more baby mantises.

What applies to male mantises used to apply to female humans. Fay Weldon wrote a wonderful book about Jane Austen, called *Letters to Alice*, and pointed out how dangerous sex used to be for women. So many died in childbirth. Which was built into the human design on purpose because two parents were only supposed to have two surviving children, to prevent us overpopulating the world. As we have done now, due to modern medicine.

So given that sex originally led to childbirth, which originally led so often to the death of the mother, why did women ever do it? Hormones. We secrete hormones which are designed to drive us mad. Hormones make us fall in love. I remember a friend telling me of the extraordinary promiscuity of her husband, and I told her sex drives people mad. That was before I found out she'd been having a long affair with her electrician, which was pretty mad as well.

But that brings me to the interesting dichotomy between the genders. Women have quite a short shelf life: we are built to fall in love, go through the menopause, become sexually unattractive and unenthusiastic, or die in childbirth. Men can go on procreating with whoever, whenever, no time limit, no matter how old they are. As a womanising celebrity (married) used to tell his temporary girlfriends, men are supposed to spread their genes around, otherwise all that sperm is wasted. However, marriage was designed to stop all that, although it clearly failed in his case. Obviously, when sex inevitably led to babies, marriage was intended to keep couples together for the sake of the children, at least in most religions in the Western world. Because there is no doubt that chil-

S

dren do far better with two parents in a stable, loving relationship.

But now that, thanks to contraception, we have separated sex from procreation, are we happier? Better adjusted? More loving? Is it progress that ten-year-olds watch pornography, that teenagers send each other naked pictures of themselves, that icons and influencers find their sex tapes posted on the internet? Have we gained our bodies, but lost our souls?

Here is the good news. When you're too old for sex, sanity returns. Here is the bad news. Then, nobody listens to you.

Incidentally, isn't it interesting that film crews now have to employ intimacy coordinators to stop graphic sex scenes hurting and embarrassing the actors involved in them? Has anybody asked cinema audiences whether they actually enjoy the sex scenes which have become way, way more graphic? Ask me which is the best sex scene I've ever seen in a movie, and I'll tell you: Meg Ryan in the cafe in *When Harry Met Sally*, when the director's mother, Estelle Reiner, said she'd have whatever Meg was having.

Sexism

I've certainly experienced it, but not in its heyday when people gloried in it, men and women alike, as if nature had intended women to be excluded from opportunity. Some of those who were most prejudiced against promoting women in those days were women. But they were a previous generation. In my time people were beginning to offer women the chances they deserved. So I was lucky.

Now as you look around the world you see terrible

examples of repression and victimisation of women. Afghanistan and Iran are setting the clock back centuries. And all done in the name of religion. Women elsewhere should do everything we can to support them. To me, that's far more important than criminalising catcalls.

Shakespeare

I don't mind how often I see productions of A *Midsummer Night's Dream*, or *Twelfth Night*; they always enchant me, but I will never again go to see a *Macbeth* or a *King Lear*. Not that they are bad plays, obviously, but watching all that blood, or an old man's eye bounce across a stage, is no longer my idea of fun. And I'm a bit dubious about *Hamlet* since going to a four-hour version, which I seem to remember included a full-frontal Kenneth Branagh. Although I may have imagined that.

The Silver Line

(See also *Loneliness*)
Sophie Andrews was the brilliant founding CEO of The Silver Line, who created a service based on friendship and empowerment. Not that she was unaware of the parameters, and the need for safeguarding, but that as a long-term Samaritan and an ex-national chair of the Samaritans she understood how to bring out the best in volunteers and respect the beneficiaries. She brought on board Anthea Beeks, who created the training for the helpline and the friendship services. Together they achieved everything we needed to provide conversation and telephone companionship and friendship, except the fundraising to pay for it.

S

That was not their fault. We discovered the hard way that older people's charities are way down the public's agenda for giving. Apart from dementia charities, there is nothing in the top 10 most popular charities relating to older people, nor in the top 20, nor in the top 30, nor in the top 40. Age UK comes in at 42. So it was unsurprising that by 2018 we realised that The Silver Line could not support itself, and we went looking for partnerships.

By chance I had arranged a meeting with Steph Harland, the CEO of Age UK, to ask about their technology. At the end of our conversation she said to me, 'How is your funding going?' I said we had enough to run for the next four weeks. She said, 'Do you need emergency funding?' And I burst into tears.

Steph fetched me some tissues, I wiped my eyes, and we talked. As a result, The Silver Line became part of Age UK.

Mergers are not easy. Having lived through the challenges Childline faced when it first became part of the NSPCC, I know it took 15 years for both organisations to make their partnership work, so that both brands could achieve the awareness and the strength they need and the most vulnerable children are supported and protected. Now the NSPCC is there for those who want to support a big overarching charity for children, and Childline is there for those who prefer a smaller niche charity.

The terrific thing about becoming part of Age UK is that The Silver Line helpline is still there, still answering older people who are desperately lonely, and the service hopefully will grow and develop as the years go by. But there are challenges, of course. Mergers are not easy.

So when small niche charities ask me about merging

with big ones, I always caution them. Do not make your-self vulnerable to asset-stripping. Make sure your service is respected and protected. And try to make sure you have some influence over the merger, so that your culture is maintained. As they always say in business, culture eats strategy for breakfast.

Smiling

Cheaper than a facelift, but just as effective at lifting cheeks and corners of the mouth. Also, maintaining the expression can persuade you that you are more cheerful than you think you are.

Smoking

I smoked 60 a day at my worst, but gave up in my early thirties. Now I can't understand why people still do it. As I have already admitted (so I must be proud of it, in spite of the violence involved), I have been known to snatch cigarettes out of young people's mouths.

Social Media

Personally, I don't bother. I have friends and relatives who keep up with each other via Facebook, and I know Twit-ter can be enormously commercially and professionally valuable if you are a loud-mouthed politician or television presenter. But the price seems to be high: they can be extremely time-consuming and sometimes vituperative and destructive. So I write emails to my friends, family and colleagues, and letters to the papers.

Staking Out

Technical term for journalists who have been stationed outside someone's home or office to take pictures or snatch an interview. If it ever happens to you, I have found a few ways to navigate it quite enjoyably.

When I was first pregnant, because I had miscarried previously, my doctor advised me to spend as much as possible of my first three months resting in bed. At which point the national press arrived at my front door. I was in my bedroom, warm, dry and resting. From my window I could see that the half-dozen stakers on my doorstep were getting cold and wet and from time to time would send one of their group off to buy a Chinese takeaway.

At which point, our musical director on *That's Life!* rang and said he needed to come and talk to me. So I explained I was being staked out. He asked how he could get past the reporters. I suggested he should stick a pencil behind his ear, a clipboard under his arm, tell them he'd come about the boiler and ring the doorbell. He did all that and got in easily. So that's one way. Stay in bed. And get your guests to pretend to be the plumber.

When *That's Life!*'s wonderful scriptwriter John Lloyd died, and I had to write our script for the first time, a *Sun* newspaper reporter was staking me out to interrogate me about something to do with my private life. He had arrived at around four in the afternoon outside the reception of our BBC building in Lime Grove. I was struggling to turn the research into a script, so I was in my office working until three in the morning. By which time the *Sun* had gone home. That's another way. Outlast them.

S

Then some nasty person, I have my suspicions who it was, started to tell the papers untruthfully that *That's Life!* was going to be axed. I got irritated, so when Chester Zoo rang to tell me their black rhinoceros named after me was pregnant, I plotted revenge on the press. (A dangerous game, ask Harry and Meghan.) So I incited my PA to ring the papers and tell them she had overheard me talking to my producer friend about the fact that, although she was aged 54, Esther was pregnant.

Ten minutes later my office phone rang: it was Desmond, in a rage. He'd had a bunch of flowers from the editor of the *Daily Mail*, saying they knew he had it in him. What had I done? I explained. He exploded. I should of course have warned him, because the press were on to him at once. What should he say? Could he say he had no information at the moment, I asked? No, of course he couldn't. Could he lie low for a day? Just so I had time to enjoy my trick. He put the phone down, still furious.

Our PA, Julia, told me later that by this time there was a group of journalists leaning against our front door, breathing on the glass and ringing the doorbell every ten minutes. Once, while she stood at the door explaining to them that everyone was out, Desi dropped something noisily in his office and they commented sarcastically about what heavy mice we had.

Eventually, Desi got bored with being imprisoned and, as he had a meeting to attend, decided he had to get away, so he wrapped a headscarf around his hair, put on an old mackintosh, took a stick and did his impression of a little old lady as he walked out through the back garden and drove off.

S

At which point I rang the director of communications at the BBC and confessed what I had done. He laughed, and then told me to tell the press the truth, otherwise he said they would never forgive me. So I went to my mother's flat, rang my home from there and asked to speak to a journalist. Julia told me the reporters wrestled with each other to get through the front door first and grab the phone, but when I spoke to one of them her voice was honey-sweet as she thanked me for speaking to them and congratulated me on the happy forthcoming event. I explained there must have been a misunderstanding, that the Esther who was pregnant was a black rhino in Chester Zoo, and the father was a black rhino called Michael Parkinson.

So the editor of the *Sunday Mirror* created a double-page spread of the two rhinos, under the headline DID THE EARTH MOVE FOR YOU, MICHAEL?

And that is the last piece of advice I have when you are being staked out: if you have a handy disguise and a back gate, do what Desi did. If not, smile, tell them as little as possible, but stick to the truth, otherwise they will never forgive you.

Swearing

(See also *Bollocks*)

I used to say to my children, I don't mind what you call me as long as it's imaginative, like calling me 'a smelly dung beetle rolling a mountain of camel manure', not an idiot. I can't say it improved their vocabulary as much as I'd hoped, but our relationship seems to have survived.

S

Tea

After the first writer-producer John Lloyd died and I began the daunting task of writing the programme, I used to ask our newest intern on *That's Life!* to fetch me '27 cups of tea'. Some thought I couldn't be serious and only brought me two or three. But I meant as many as would fit on a tray. And I drank them as I wrote, to blast some kind of creativity into my brain.

Now, when I speak to isolated older people who have rung The Silver Line helpline, very often they say all they really want is somebody to come and visit for a cup of tea and a chat. Putting the kettle on is the generally accepted gesture of companionship, of welcome. Coffee is a bit more edgy and sophisticated. Tea is homely.

And the impact of tea can be magic. My parents used to recite to me 'the cup that cheers but does not inebriate', which seems to be a misquote from an eighteenth-century poem. Maybe it's the caffeine in it, maybe it's the tannin, maybe it's just magic. But there is no doubt that it revives you if you're shocked or traumatised, it inspires you if there's a challenging task to be done, and it's the perfect way to start the day. Especially if someone else brings it to you in bed.

But there has been a revolution in the way we drink tea. Bags have taken over from the dried flakes of leaf we used to douse in boiling water in a teapot, taking the 'pot to the kettle, not the kettle to the pot' to ensure the water stayed hot enough to brew properly. And when we finished our cup, there in the bottom was a collection of tea leaves we used to swirl around and then consult to see what future it prophesied for us. No prophets can consult a teabag, except I suppose to admit that they are very difficult, sometimes impossible, to recycle. Another danger progress has created for our fragile planet.

But who really knows what the future will bring, what havoc may hit the world in decades to come? No crystal ball, no astrological arrangements of the stars and planets, and certainly no tea leaves warned us about climate change. It was the independent scientist James Lovelock, with his books about Gaia, who predicted that the world in balance, the earth's crucial self-regulation system, has been knocked askew by human interference. Alas, as each year proves to be hotter than the last, it may take more than a comforting cup of tea to protect humanity in the years to come.

T

My A–Z of surviving almost everything

Tech

It is intimidating to some of us. So, like maths, it's a good idea to employ someone who enjoys mending it when it goes wrong. Which it does. But don't let that put you off. It is worrying that some people, especially older people, find the digital world too anxiety-provoking even to start to explore it. Yes, there are dangers, just as there are in any new adventure, but they are not overwhelming. Nor are the skills you will need completely out of reach: if you can type, you can use a computer. And once you set out on it, the internet will take you into fabulous new worlds and answer any question you care to pose.

So don't allow yourself to be cut off, or refuse to learn technology's little ways because at first you may find it unfamiliar and therefore uncomfortable. Like any new language, like learning to drive a car, it will be worth it.

Telephone

An old-fashioned piece of technology that brings people together and enables them to ask for help safely and anonymously. Many helplines, such as Samaritans, Childline and The Silver Line, rely upon it. But the telephone has transformed over the last 50 years. It used to be a piece of furniture tethered to a plug in the wall; now it is mobile and a constant companion. Its strength used to be that the human voice can communicate not only facts, but also how we feel. But when I asked a group of young people around ten years ago whether they preferred to talk or text on their phones, unanimously they chose texting.

T

So I wonder how the telephone will have morphed, in another ten years? I do hope it will still offer the safety, the warmth, the anonymity that has made the telephone such a valuable lifeline.

Television

Like all popular pieces of technology, television has changed so much during my lifetime. I remember a small box with a flickering black-and-white picture that reduced to a white dot when you turned it off. Now people have created cinemas in their basements to watch enormous, brightly coloured pictures beamed into them from around the world. And instead of the one channel, we now have hundreds to choose from. So has that improved our choice?

Once, and I made programmes in this era, everyone watched the same shows and we all shared what were known as 'water-cooler moments'. Our series *That's Life!* created any number of such moments with talking dogs and ping-pong-playing cats. And campaigns like Ben Hardwick. Could you reach audiences of 18-20 million today with those? I think not.

Tastes are so disparate nowadays (see *Beliefs and Tribalism*). The BBC has been lambasted for appealing to the middle classes. Well, somebody has to. And it's not just a matter of class. There are very few programmes that appeal across every age group, either. I can't cope with the so-called reality shows, which they say young viewers love but which show anything but reality, relying on fame-hungry participants competing and then being trolled viciously when they get back into real life. Nor can I feast on a diet of true crime, the more violent and nasty the more popular, that some channels seem to rely upon for big audiences. There are still programmes which showcase skills like painting, or restoring and repairing, or cooking, or assessing antiques, or answering quiz questions, and many of them are well-crafted and presented, but whether the young enjoy them as much as we oldies do, I cannot say.

I implore broadcasters not to throw everything into trying to attract the 16–24 year olds. (There actually used to be stickers on BBC lifts printed with 16-24!) But the young should have much better ways of spending their time than watching TV. The viewers who rely on television for company and mental stimulation are the isolated older people. So please don't dump them, I beg you.

That's Life!

In May 1973 the BBC launched a consumer programme which went on to top the TV ratings and run for 21 years. It was a strange hybrid show, based on viewers' lives, with a large studio audience, jokes, music, and tough investigations. In its 21 years it changed laws and attitudes, saved lives, sent conmen to jail and created a group of TV professionals who still call themselves 'Lifers'. Many people recall it as the only show they were allowed to stay up and watch on Sunday nights, because although it was naughty (rude vegetables) it was also nice (consumer advice).

Axed in 1994, it has never been replaced. People have tried, but unsurprisingly failed: it never was an easy show to make. So aspects of it have been picked off, the talented animals for instance, and the consumer advice. Every now and then a show arrives on the air with a flavour of *That's Life!* (Joe Lycett has one at the moment). But nothing has its range, from how to save the life of a toddler with biliary atresia to a talking dog.

What gave it special clout was its enormous viewing audience, at its peak over 22 million. But of course, these days streaming can achieve similar ratings worldwide. And have similar influence, which is why autocratic governments do everything they can to control the internet and dictate what their population is allowed to watch.

Can a viral video have the influence *That's Life!* once had? Yes, indeed. But will that video be remembered with the affection and nostalgia *That's Life!*'s production team and many viewers feel for our strange show? I'd be surprised.

Theatre

When it's good it's very, very good.

When it's bad it's unbearable.

Time

So stretchy. Looking backwards it seems to have flashed by. Where did those years disappear to? But we can all remember when we were children and an hour took a lifetime to pass. Trying to get to sleep on a sunny evening took an eternity. Waking in the middle of the night before Christmas, how long did it take for the moment to come when you were allowed to explore the deliciously lumpy stocking Santa had left you on your eiderdown? If, as we grow older, we can slow down the hands of our clocks, enjoy each tiny moment, that must be the way to value the time we're given. If.

Tribalism

People used to be able to disagree in a friendly way with a political opponent or listen with interest to someone with profoundly different views from their own. Nowadays it seems we have to cancel speakers with different views, or pile vitriol onto them via the internet. Looking across the world, passion and fury divide countries from each other. And religions. And politics and culture. If we're right, they must be totally wrong (see *Beliefs*).

The truth is that unless humanity learns to collaborate, to understand how we can survive together and ensure that we do, we will surely disappear off the face of the earth. Tribalism may have protected us as a hominid. But it will surely condemn us as a species.

So how do we protect ourselves against tribalism? Listen and learn, I suppose.

Umbrella

I may have mentioned my theory that no experience is wasted. For example, when I did a 'secretarial course' after university, although I can't say advice like, 'always keep a spare silk stocking in your handbag in case of a ladder' was much help, it was incredibly useful to be taught to touch type.

My two-and-a-half years spent working in BBC radio making sound effects are another good example. You may think that there was not much point in my being trained to click coconut shells to make the sound of trotting horses. Or in my knowing how to make recording tape and soggy pillows rustle together like the feet of lovers walking in a muddy autumn meadow. But one day you might like to make the flapping sound of a low-flying pterodactyl, and if you do, I recommend you run around with a very large umbrella, opening and shutting it as you run. Fortunately, even if that doesn't sound exactly

My A–Z of surviving almost everything

like a pterodactyl, there's nobody still alive who can contradict you.

University

When I was a student, it was understood that you were not adult until you were 21. There was a song about getting the key of the door at that age. So university tutors knew they were *in loco parentis* for their 18, 19, 20-year-old students. Not any more.

For obvious reasons, politicians who believed the young would support them and vote for them have dropped the age of official adulthood to 18. Sometimes 16. And yet neurologists now recognise that our brains don't mature until we are 25 and the cerebral wires connect up. So looked-after children remain the responsibility of the local authority up to the age of 25. Rightly.

But universities still pretend their undergraduates are adults. I believe there are suicides happening in universities that could and should be prevented if they intervened to ensure that their students were being properly supported emotionally. The late teens are a time of maximum emotional vulnerability. You can get more depressed, more anxious then than at any other time, as most of us would remember from our own lives. And if loneliness strikes, or a feeling of inadequacy or inferiority makes student life unbearable, the university staff should spot it and intervene.

And as a first crucial step, they should make public the number of young lives lost. The only way to deal with a problem, and this is a serious problem, is to admit it, and map and measure it.

It's not good enough to be judged on academic success. You must do more, universities, to take responsibility for, and to take care of, your most precious assets, the young people entrusted to you.

Seven Fairly Useful Tips and Life Hacks

- A pain in the neck
  If you get neck ache, check your position when you're watching television. I used to curl up in a comfortable chair, and a physiotherapist told me that was why I had a recurring pain. She said I must sit straight, look straight ahead. And magically, when I followed her advice, the pain evaporated. Except when I watched *Love Island*.

U

My A–Z of surviving almost everything

- Hosting

  You may love holding dinner parties. I applaud you. But I gave up when I became single again. Instead, I have two dozen friends who meet once a month in a local restaurant, splitting the bill evenly between us, not noticing whether we all had pudding, or drank more than our fair share of wine. With one proviso. One friend used to arrive half an hour before the rest of us, and spent that extra time guzzling champagne cocktails, making sure their price was added to the bill the rest of us shared. And he used to leave just before the bill arrived, contributing a few bank notes which didn't nearly cover the cost of his drinks, let alone his food. So I stopped inviting him.

- Christmas decorations

  My daughter Rebecca has inherited her father Desmond's love of celebrations, especially everything surrounding Christmas. Each December she decorates her home with holly and tinsel and lights and trees and wreaths and baubles and offers this crucial tip. If you share her desire to make every inch of wall space and mantelpiece celebratory, before you take it all down again, she advises you to take a picture of it in all its finery, and then pack the stuff away, clearly labelled, in a box per room.

- Laundry

  Put a device to hang wet laundry next to your washing machine to save you having to roam around with a basket in your arms. And if you can afford it, have your sweaters dry-cleaned. Specially the

U

cashmeres. Even when the washing instructions claim they can survive, they often can't.

- Panettone is delicious if you microwave it for about ten seconds. And, if you like, add cream.

- Always wash up dishes in the sink the night before. It's nasty to come down to dirty crockery in the morning, and food gets encrusted.

- Plump up the cushions before you go to bed: that's known as the '*Hello!* touch'. Before their photographers take a picture of you relaxing at home, they also walk around plumping up the cushions so it looks smart in the background.

Vegetables, Vegetarians and Vegans

Some people, usually men in my experience, don't like eating vegetables. I love them. And I've found as one grows older one likes them more, and red meat less. So I sympathise with people whose diet relies less on steak and more on quinoa, whatever that is and however it's pronounced (see *Food*).

I understand why people become vegetarian, but vegans are at the extreme edge of plant-eating and animal-product-avoiding, so although I admire their passion they go further than I can emulate. Especially as I adore caviar, which I'm sure they prohibit.

I remember my husband Desmond was alarmed when I told him I was going to cook our wedding breakfast after our second wedding ceremony, when we arrived at our country cottage in the New Forest. He was relieved when I revealed that it just meant my making toast, hard boiling eggs for their yolks, chopping an onion and opening a jar of capers and two tins of beluga caviar. Fiendishly expensive but delicious.

So I couldn't become a vegan. Sorry, sturgeons.

Victoria Wood

When I first worked in television as a researcher on a chat show, the joke was that each week we'd start by mentally booking the impossible guest. 'If not the queen, Charlie Chaplin'. But by the time each show was actually made, we were grateful for whoever happened to come along because they had a book to plug. When eventually I became a presenter myself, my dream guest was neither the queen nor Charlie Chaplin, but Victoria Wood, and one wonderful evening that dream came true.

It was around thirty years ago when a Childline fundraiser rang me at home, thrilled, to tell me, 'Victoria Wood says she'll do a show for us, Esther, if you will interview her.' I didn't hesitate for a heartbeat. 'Of course I will.' 'One snag,' he said. 'It's in a hall in Ilkley.' 'Fine,' I said. So it meant a three hour drive there and the same back in an evening? Fine. Frankly, if it had been in Reykjavik it would still have been fine.

Victoria asked me to ring her the Sunday before, just to check out the question line. 'What are you going to ask me about?' she said. I knew the basic facts of her life, and I took her through the chapters, the lonely childhood, the lack of confidence, her love of music, our first meeting on *That's Life!* and then her huge success in every genre, and each time she gave the telephone equivalent of a nod. I put the phone down and realised that I had been quite nervous. I admired her so much.

V

I always had, right from the moment she won the talent show *New Faces*. At that time I was a regular on the Radio 4 show *Start the Week* with Richard Baker, and for a while she sang songs on that programme and I was entranced with this shy, young, totally original musician, so we booked her on *That's Life!* I have already quoted her saying about that time, 'I don't know why they go on about her teeth, have you seen her dresses?' Which was fair.

The night of the Childline show arrived; I emerged from my car in Ilkley after the three-hour drive, feeling like a sardine still crumpled from its tin. Victoria was nowhere in sight, although I did hear some soft sounds from the dressing room next to mine. When I was summoned up to the stage Vicky was standing in the wings, very quiet: she gave me a smile. I walked on to moderate applause from an audience crammed into every cranny, hanging off railings; the little hall was packed to the rafters. I introduced Victoria, the place exploded, and on she came, now radiant, as if lit up from within by her own energy and talent. And then I had the professional experience of my life. I will never forget sitting next to her, asking a few questions and listening to her turn her life into the most perfectly crafted anecdotes, each one with a hilarious tag. She had needed all her quiet concentration to muster up that amazing, polished performance. I just wish I had recorded it.

During the interval she relaxed and we chatted. And then in the second half she answered questions from the audience, again pulling out of the air the most wonderful tag lines. The show ended, she disappeared with some friends for a quiet curry, and I went back down the motorway, reliving every moment of that dream interview.

Of course I've seen her since, live in the Albert Hall, where I believe she holds the record for the number of sell-out shows, and marvelled at the artistry of that little woman: no funny props, no feathers or sequins, just her piano to keep her company. And every time she held that giant Albert Hall audience in the palm of her hand, just as she had in Ilkley. What a writer. What a performer. (If you doubt me, just try singing 'The Ballad of Barry and Freda' at the tongue-twisting speed she manages.) What a genius. Why was she never Dame-d for her talent? I don't know. How did she stay so real, so grounded, that her wit and observation stayed truthful, not spiteful, just funny and insightful? I can't say. Would I rather have interviewed the queen or Charlie Chaplin? Absolutely not. I am thrilled to be able to boast that I have sat next to and interviewed Victoria Wood, and watched her turn the story of her life, and all our lives, into a work of art.

V

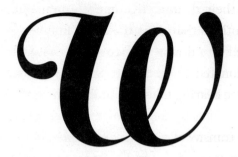

Wet Wet Wet

In 1988, when Childline was newly launched, an album arrived on my desk at the BBC. The *New Musical Express* had created a cover version of the Beatles' masterpiece *Sgt. Pepper's Lonely Hearts Club Band* using contemporary bands, and decided to donate the profits from the sales to Childline.

We listened to all the tracks and two particularly stood out: 'With a Little Help From My Friends', by a Scottish band I hadn't heard of called Wet Wet Wet, and 'She's Leaving Home' by Billy Bragg. We decided to feature them both on the programme.

In those days the BAFTAs were a hugely popular and prestigious television event, so we were chagrined that year that they were being shown on ITV, directly opposite our programme. We knew not many viewers would choose to watch us rather than them. What we didn't know was that among our viewers would be Wet Wet Wet themselves, and their drummer, Tommy Cunningham, suggested to the others that their track and Billy Bragg's should be released as a double A-side single, with their royalties being donated to Childline. So their publicist arrived in our office bearing that wonderful news, and we told our viewers.

The result was transformational for Childline. The disc rocketed to the top of the charts and stayed at number one for four weeks. Those were the days when records sold in millions, and the money raised paid for Childline to open a base in Glasgow.

Wet Wet Wet never forgot the connection and used to hold collections for Childline at all their concerts. I happened to be visiting our Childline base in Manchester when they held a concert there. They very kindly gave me a pass to meet them backstage, and while I was talking to them, a singer from another boy band turned up. I was struck by his charisma and vitality: it was Robbie Williams from Take That. He told Marty Pellow how much he envied the Wets' freedom, because he said his group was so much more regimented, instructed in exactly how and what they had to perform.

The very next day Robbie announced he was leaving Take That. Marty and I have discussed it since, and wondered how much the creative freedom Robbie watched during Wet Wet Wet's concert that night had spurred him to leave his highly successful group.

W

Cynics are sometimes scathing about celebrities supporting charities. My experience has been entirely positive. By spreading awareness and raising funds, the celebrities give so much back. Certainly Wet Wet Wet did.

Winton, Sir Nicholas

It was an unforgettable phone call from my friend Eve Pollard (Claudia Winkleman's mother and a distinguished newspaper editor), in 1988, who alerted me to one of the most moving stories I have heard, and we ever told, on *That's Life!*

Eve explained to me that the Wintons, a married couple living near Maidenhead, had been decluttering their loft when they came across an album filled with documents and photographs. Nicholas Winton explained to his wife that they belonged to Czech Jewish children who had been rescued just in time from the Nazi invasion and brought to England. He had put together a rescue team, organised the operation and found British families to foster the children. Then for 50 years he had never talked about it.

We examined the album, which contained the lists of children, and our researcher began trying to track them. I remember my first phone call with Nicky Winton. I congratulated him on the wonderful achievement of saving more than 600 lives, but he said to me, 'It was not enough.' He told me of the last train standing in the station in Prague in 1939, filled with more than 200 children, and the Gestapo then invaded Czechoslovakia and shut the borders, so all the children were taken off the train and disappeared, doubtless murdered in concentration camps. Clearly, that memory broke his heart.

We agreed to help him track them down and return the documents and pictures to the survivors, probably the only souvenirs they would ever have of their childhood. On the Sunday night of our show we invited Nicky to

W

the studio, to 'check we got our facts right', put him in the front row of the audience and infuriated him by not allowing him to sit next to his wife. It took years for him to forgive me, if ever. But of course we wanted to seat him next to the people he had saved as children, although they knew nothing about him, and he didn't recognise them.

When the programme started, I made sure the camera showed as many names as possible as I turned over the pages of the album. I reminded viewers of the enormous courage of the parents who had put their children on those trains, not knowing what would happen to them. I told the story of one child, Vera Gissing, and then revealed to Vera and Nicky that they were sitting next to each other. She hugged him and thanked him for her life. Watching them, it was the only time I had to stop recording, silenced by my own tears. I still weep every time I watch that moment.

After that programme we were contacted by dozens of people who had recognised the names we had shown, and we invited them back to our studio. This time, we sat Nicky in the front row next to his wife. We told more stories of the children whose lives he had saved, and then I asked everyone who owed their life to Nicky to stand. He heard a rustle behind him, turned round and saw the whole of the audience on the ground floor of the television theatre on their feet. You can watch that moment immortalised on the internet.

The legacy of his extraordinary achievement lives on. Not least because one of 'Winton's Children', as they became known, is Alfred Dubs. Lord Dubs was responsible for the Dubs Amendment, which gives unaccompanied refugee children the right to join families in Britain.

W

Nicky was knighted for his achievement, and honoured around the world, especially in the Czech Republic. I remember seeing video of a conference he was invited to in Prague where thousands of young people were asked to light up their phones if his example showing how much difference one person could make had inspired them to action, and thousands of phones lit up. Nicky was clearly deeply moved. That was the legacy he most wanted to leave.

He believed that history is pointless unless we learn from it, and do not repeat terrible tragedies like the Holocaust. He never referred to 'the Holocaust' because he believed there have been many before and since: Rwanda, for example. I am so relieved he didn't live to see the terrible destruction and murder in Ukraine.

I admired him enormously. We remained friends and lunched together regularly. He died at the age of 106 and I spoke at his memorial service. On the spur of the moment I asked the people there to stand if they owed their lives to him, and once again practically everyone in the hall stood up.

Some advice I can pass on from Nicky: he had decided at the age of 90 never to turn down an invitation to do something he had never done before. Although he told me that when he went up in a microlight piloted by one of the 'Winton's Children' children, to celebrate his 100th birthday, it was extremely draughty up his trouser legs.

W
___

Women

Some of my best friends are, two of my daughters are, I am one myself, so I know exactly what they are, but I don't intend to hazard a definition because for some reason that incites fury among those who disagree.

The rage seems to centre around trans people, which is strange because the trans people themselves seem to be far less enraged, although often deeply distressed by the humiliation and bullying they have experienced.

I have made several programmes about trans people and have met a very young trans person, as I recall around ten years old, born a girl but definite that she/he was in the wrong body, and was in fact a boy. Mum was helpless, longing to know how to help, but not knowing what to do for the best.

I told this story to a feminist, who seemed convinced that the child must in fact have been a lesbian. Which was absolutely not what the child thought or said, she/he said she/he was a boy. And was deeply distressed to be in the wrong body. The only support the mother told me they'd had was from the charity Mermaids, much reviled in the press.

So whatever you think women are, I agree with you.

Wrinkles

They creep up on you. Especially if you follow current medical advice and get thinner as you grow older. A little extra plumpness stops the skin creasing too badly. And taking your glasses off when you look in the mirror helps. Knee wrinkles are the most unexpected and irritating for those of us trained by the sixties to enjoy miniskirts, which

W

are now out of bounds to us. Can one have a knee-lift? According to the internet you can, but it doesn't sound much fun or particularly effective. Unlike facelifts, which work extremely well until they don't.

W
___

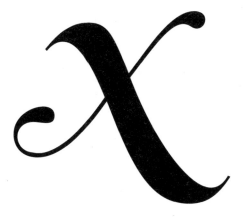

X-husbands, wives and girl/boyfriends

Looking back, what were we thinking of?

X-rays

There used to be X-ray machines in every shoe shop so that children could have their feet X-rayed to see how much room there was in their shoes. Nowadays, dentists hide behind a screen whenever they take an X-ray of our mouths. If our feet drop off, we will know why.

You

Take care of yourself – you need you. Not what you do: who you are.

As a baby, and then a child, if you are lucky enough to be loved and looked after, you feel you exist as a person, not just judged by what you do or work at. But for most of the rest of our lives we are defined by our function. From the moment you go to school you become a pupil, then a student, then perhaps a partner or a spouse, then a parent, a grandparent, and in old age a pensioner, or even more judgementally, a house-blocker or a bed-blocker. And that's without being additionally judged by whatever your job label may be.

Somehow while you are juggling all the responsibilities of these functions and roles you can get lost as the person you once were. So I recommend that you consciously insert into your life, for at least half a day each week, moments when you indulge yourself. Perhaps not with something potentially addictive and destructive like drink, drugs or gambling which could take over all the rest of your life and your family's life. But something the real you enjoys and which energises you, like a stroll, or an absorbing book to read, or someone fun to phone. Because there may come a time when all the other functions fall away, and you are left with what people call 'your hinterland'. And if you haven't been there since you were four, that can be quite intimidating. As I have said, the killer question for many older people is 'What do you do for fun?' And far too many of them cannot remember.

Zimmer Frames

My husband Desmond died on a Tuesday. On the Friday I had been booked by Samaritans to speak in York at a conference for their volunteers. I decided to go, even though, as you will imagine, the world had turned on its axis. My son kindly went with me.

I started my speech by thanking the Samaritans for inviting me and saving me the cost of a phone call. Being kindly people, they laughed. I ended with an anecdote about their founder, Chad Varah, whom I had met and chatted with at the conference hall reception. He was using a Zimmer frame. I mentioned that my mother used one too. 'In that case,' Chad said, 'she's probably got the same condition I have.' I didn't contradict him, although it was unlikely, as she had an ovarian cyst. The Samaritans laughed at that, too. Actually, when she was leaning on hers in a supermarket, it ran away with her and she landed on the floor with a fractured hip. So if you are using a Zimmer on wheels, beware.

Zoo

Children love them, but do animals? At least they have improved since the dreary, depressing Victorian cages we used to visit in London Zoo as children, where miserable wolves used to pace around the barred walls, doubtless wondering what crime they had committed to be punished like this.

But occasionally the animals took their revenge. My mother used to be an adenoidal child. She was once taken to the zoo and was standing in front of the monkey cage with her mouth open, as usual, when one of the monkeys took aim and peed straight into it. She never forgot the sensation of warm liquid on her tongue. My grandmother was a serene soul: instead of panicking, she went over to a vending machine, bought a bar of chocolate, and gave it to my mother to take the taste away.

Serenity is a great gift.

Z

___

Zoom

And Facetime, and Instagram.

Technology exploits us, so let's exploit it, using it to reach out to the people and activities that enrich our lives. Don't bother with the people we dislike, or who dislike us. Stick with the people whose company we enjoy, who make us laugh, and energise us. I have many friends who tell me they 'don't do Zoom'. But I do. And I find that it's got all the advantages of company without the commuting. So enjoy.

Z
___

Outro

A nd there you have it: my A–Z of survival. I'm sure you will have disagreed with me from time to time, but I hope there will be something that resonates with you. If it inspires or provokes you to write your own A–Z, so much the better. You'll find it's great fun to assemble your prejudices and let rip, because why worry whether anyone else approves? You have earned the right to your own views. Remember: history is written by the survivors, be bolder as you grow older, and make sure you float above any challenges that threaten to overwhelm you.

As Scarlett O'Hara taught us: no matter how tough yesterday was, and maybe today still is, tomorrow is another day.

Afterword

A nd that, I thought, was that. I'd put together every significant memory I had collected over my 82 years, or at least the memories that I am prepared to share with you, dear reader. I'd had great fun rifling through them all, extracting the life lessons I'd learned, and failed to learn, over the years and putting them in alphabetical order for you.

So finally, to round it off, I called upon my inner Scarlett O'Hara, with her indomitable faith in tomorrow, quoted her, drew a line and sent it off to my lovely publisher, Lorna Russell. And a couple of days later I looked at my reflection in the mirror as I got dressed, thought, *That's an interesting lump in my armpit – maybe I've been bitten by something. Why don't I show it to the doctor?* and did.

And suddenly a whole new chapter in my life began. With many, many new lessons to learn. Which, at the time of writing, I am still learning. So it turns out that I, who thought I knew everything, in fact knew nothing.

It all started quite quietly. When I showed my armpit to her, my GP reassured me that it was probably a cyst, but said as a matter of routine she would refer me to a 'one-stop shop' breast cancer clinic in our excellent local hospital. That was on a Thursday. So I spent a happy weekend with my daughter and her family, thinking nothing of it.

Monday came, and I went for my appointment at the breast clinic. There I was introduced to a consultant, who drew a biro circle around the lump and sent me next door for a mammogram (clear) and a biopsy. The radiologist who did the biopsy was wearing a mask, so I don't know what she looked like, but I could tell she was very expert and distinguished. She dug a large hole in some lymph nodes she found and told me there were more than one, so I knew it wasn't a cyst. And back I went to the consultant, who said, slightly apologetically, that he wanted me to have a full-body CT scan next. Used to cameras as I am, that was fine with me. And the scan revealed that I have lung cancer, which has spread here and there, including my armpit.

Two irritating things about that. Firstly, as you will have noticed, I am an evangelical non-smoker, prone to snatching cigarettes from the mouths of young people I don't know. I gave up smoking myself 50 years ago, so all the health educators told me I had a brand new pair of lungs. However, it turns out there are other kinds of lung cancer which are not smoking related. And I've got one of those. Which will teach me not to be so smug and self-righteous.

The other thing I learned was that one scan leads to another. And while you wait for the results from each one, there is a condition that attacks you called Scanxiety. Every day you have to wait for the results feels like a year. And in my case, each scan revealed something else substandard somewhere on my body, most of which I must have lived with for decades and nobody cared about. But it made me take my long-suffering body less for granted.

The biopsy was the main piece of evidence we had to wait for, the lump that the distinguished radiologist had gouged out of my armpit. To discover exactly what I was suffering from depended upon that biopsy, and it took ages and ages (three weeks or so, which felt like 30 years) to come up with the answer. Which was that my lung cancer is a rare kind, not smoking related, a variety which most commonly attacks young Asian women, and can be treated. Not cured. But held back.

I was astonished. Turns out I know nothing about lung cancer. I thought I did. I have friends who, alas, have died of it. You probably have, too. And there have been famous sufferers, including in the royal family. So I assumed it was an instant death sentence for me, and decided I would probably be gone before next Thursday. I looked up the nearest hospice (wonderful places, hospices: they deserve all the support we can give them) and began to discuss flights to Switzerland just in case Dignitas would have room for me. And when someone taking a food order from me, which I was putting on my M&S credit card, asked me for my expiry date, I nearly said, 'In a week or two.' But restrained myself.

The question then was: who to tell? Obviously my children had to know, and they told my grandchildren, and I told my closest friends, and my sister Scilla, who lives in Australia. She and I have always been best friends. Since Covid we have been WhatsApping each other every day. Especially as we had both separately decided that the 26-hour flight to visit each other had become too difficult, she having had her health issues too. But when I told her my diagnosis she said she and her lovely husband Tony were considering coming over to stay with me. I was overjoyed at the idea. So she did.

Major, major lesson. If someone is important to you, spend time with them. Nothing else compares with that. I have colleagues who say that the crucial thing in their life is their work and that they want to drop dead working. I admire them for it, but that has never been my ambition. I've been incredibly lucky: my work has been fun, exciting and rewarding. But happiness is what counts for me; I want to die happy, and happiness means the company of my nearest and dearest. So cancer has taught me a crucial lesson. Prioritise.

Who else to tell? On my way to one of the scans in the hospital I was recognised in a lift by another patient. Admittedly, she thought I was Angela Rippon, but that was fairly close, and I was flattered. But it made me realise that one way or another the news would leak, probably inaccurately. And I've learned that trying to keep a secret never works. It just means that you are caught unprepared and on the back foot. Far better to break a piece of news yourself.

So with the help of my brilliant assistant, Julia, I sent messages to my extended family, and my beloved friends and colleagues, and the people I had depended upon for company and support over the years, warning them all that I was about to put out a statement and asking them to send me memories of the fun we had shared together. The statement said:

In the last few weeks I have discovered that I am suffering from lung cancer, which has now spread. At the moment I am undergoing various tests to assess the best treatment.

I have decided not to keep this secret anymore because I find it difficult to skulk around various hospitals wearing an unconvincing disguise, and because I would rather you heard the facts from me.

At the age of 82, this diagnosis has prompted me to look back over the years, and I want to express my profound thanks to everyone who has made my life so joyful, filled with fun and with inspiration. First and foremost, my family. My three children, Miriam, Rebecca and Joshua, have been the most wonderful support, company and source of love and laughter, and I am deeply grateful to them and to my whole family. My friends have been amazing and have created memories which sustain me and give me strength. My colleagues, with whom I have worked, and continue to work, in broadcasting, journalism, the voluntary sector and in many other organisations, have been a constant plea-sure, and have amazed me with their tolerance of my wild ideas and awful jokes.

As I am sure you will understand, while I am awaiting the results of the tests, I am unable to answer questions. Thanks to the extraordinary skills of the medical profession there are wonder-ful new treatments, so I am remaining optimistic.

Oh my goodness. The response has been overwhelming. The joy of hearing from acquaintances and old friends, and roaring with laughter at their wicked memories of our times together, has been so cheering. Another lesson cancer has taught me: the one thing worth hoarding is friendship. Never let it go. Stay in touch.

And be grateful. I have a long list of the guardian angels who have gathered around me, never asking difficult questions about my health or sanity, but just working out what support would be helpful. They include my brilliant publisher Lorna Russell and Joel Stewart our fabulous illustrator, my assistants Julia Mitchell and Victoria Swain, my agents Jackie Gill and Luigi Bonomi and their teams, my advisors Simon Robinson and Christopher Seddon, my doctors including Dr Jonathan Sheldon (the GP I left when I moved permanently to the New Forest but who has stayed in touch), my neighbours, David Sherman who turns my garden into a paradise, James Gardiner whose brilliant driving gets me to all those appointments, Natalie and Emma who make my home a very pleasant place, Natalia who cooks like a dream, my lovely friends in the dining club called 'Hamsters', my cousin Sarah, my dear friends Bryher and Paul Scudamore and Michael Bowen, my wonderful sister Priscilla Taylor and Tony who travelled 12,000 miles to provide support for me and those close to me, and above all my children Rebecca, Joshua and Miriam and their partners and children who are constantly there when and where I need them. I've been turned upside down by events, and they all have helped me regain my balance. I cannot sufficiently thank them.

As it turns out, what Samuel Johnson said about knowing you are to be hanged in two weeks also applies to a diagnosis of lung cancer, it does concentrate the mind wonderfully. However, you do occasionally need distraction, and for taking my mind off a conveyor belt of ever-changing decisions and plans, I would like to thank Wordle, BBC Sounds, Martin Jarvis reading P.G. Wodehouse, and Boots the cat who adopted us and now rules the household.

So here's what I've learned, Scarlett. Tomorrow may not be another day. There will come a time when today will be your last. So under no circumstances waste each day you are given.

Dogs have owners, cats have servants,
and I know my place.